Christology with
LONERGAN AND BALTHASAR

KEVIN TORTORELLI, O.F.M

Published by

MELROSE BOOKS

An Imprint of Melrose Press Limited
St Thomas Place, Ely
Cambridgeshire
CB7 4GG, UK
www.melrosebooks.com

FIRST EDITION

Cover design by Goeff Hobbs Design

ISBN 1 905226 13 6

Printed and bound in Great Britain by:
Bath Press Limited, Lower Bristol Road,
Bath, BA2 3BL, UK

CONTENTS

INTRODUCTION

Nowadays a book devoted to Christology takes its place in a crowded field. The present book is no exception. Many of these books are specialized exercises in exegesis or in the history of doctrine. They are deeply learned. By contrast, my book is a collection of brief essays. For this reason something more should be said about its structure and contents.

These fifteen essays represent about as many years of reading and thinking, of research and teaching in the subject of Christology. Early on they took shape as part of a course in Christology for Carthusian monks preparing for ordination. The essays have since undergone a number of revisions. In something like their present form they were offered as a series of theological lectures at the Catholic Center, The University of Georgia, Athens, in the winter and spring, 1994. In the interim, they have undergone still further revisions.

On all points these essays make no claim to being exhaustive or even complete. In them I have tried to state my critical understanding of the chief issues in Christology. In the present work, my reading of Lonergan and Balthasar has helped me identify those issues and limit their number. These issues have provided the titles of each essay. They may in fact be read in any order though preferably as arranged here. In writing and revising I found myself repeatedly encountering questions of my own authenticity: What is the evidence for such and such a view? Have I got it right? Am I sure? What difference does it make? I very much hope these essays reflect this twofold sense of a process that strives to be authentic and of a set truths that are its fruit.

By now, it will perhaps be clear that two men have had the greatest influence on me. They are Bernard Lonergan and Hans Urs Von Balthasar. They are both to be found in these pages with perhaps a slight emphasis on Lonergan. I first met him at Boston College in 1976. In the classroom, he was always demanding, occasionally bewildering. It took me years to wrap my mind round him but I have never regretted the effort. The results are by now an inevitable part of my thinking and writing. His vision is vast, unexpectedly rhapsodic and I have often enough been left breathless by its range, its coherence, even its simplicity. By contrast, I had never met Fr. Balthasar, but I well recall my first impressions on reading him. I found daunting his massive, magisterial learning and the simple confidence of his writing. His formidable text never got lost though it moved constantly over enormous detail.

One may well ask why these two theologians? Why not someone else? To an extent, I had no control over the matter. I was exposed to Lonergan first and then, by sheer contrast, I can only say I rather stumbled on Balthasar while reading St. Irenaeus. Classics and patristics had been longstanding interests. At some point, I found myself being stamped by these two men. In their writings they seemed kindred spirits with their reverence for the human spirit in the presence of God. And they each seemed good for the other. Lonergan adds a sharp focus to one's reading of Balthasar: What am I doing when I know? Why is doing that knowing? What do I know when I do it? For his part, Balthasar adds to one's reading of Lonergan a wide-ranging breadth of historical and literary detail. This texture, verdant and luxurious, is like a cozy fire after the bracing and rarified air of Lonergan. Above all, I have wanted to avoid merely juxtaposing them. This would serve no useful purpose. Rather, I wanted to bring them together under several themes to see them interact. But it should also be said that the present work is in no sense a general introduction to their thought for which one would have to look elsewhere. In this book, shortcomings are entirely my own, but I very much hope mere juxtaposing is not one of them.

From time to time, I have wondered how best to characterize these two theologians. They do not seem to have known each other or read each other. In fact their works read very differently. The one has the happy circumstance of writing clearly and tightly in lean English prose. His style is unmistakable. The other is deeply literary, biblical and historical in a recognizable continental tradition. I take the view, however, that they possess a unity that is also to be found in the Catholic intellectual tradition. In particular, I believe Lonergan and Balthasar converge and form a unity at several points in their understanding of St. Thomas Aquinas.[1] The final essay in this collection aims to illustrate that claim. To my mind, their achievement is monumental and one wonders if we shall ever see their like again.

The goal of this book is the understanding of Jesus Christ these two theologians offer. Yet the book is not a study of the Christology either of Lonergan or of Balthasar. As essays, the book is composed of meditations on the mystery of Christ in the spirit of these two theologians. It is divided into three parts, somewhat along historical lines. All citations from Scripture are taken from the New Revised Standard Version as are the abbreviations of the biblical books. This book envisions a readership with a broad theological interest and background. It will, I think, benefit undergraduates and be of particular interest to graduate students. Others may have read independently to that level and I believe the book will be useful to them as well.

In that spirit, I hope the essays set the reader to thinking and help one fashion a response to the question that does not go away – who do you say I am?

PART I

ESSAY ONE: SOURCES AND METHODS

Scripture is the privileged source for our knowledge of Jesus. Historically, how has Scripture been approached so as to disclose its meaning? How do you understand Scripture? The meaning of Scripture is especially important as it witnesses to the formal Revelation of God.

The various methods of understanding are gathered in the term hermeneutics. Here I simply mean the rules and practice of interpretation. Sometimes one finds hermeneutics reserved for the science and theory of interpretation while exegesis is its art and practice, but this distinction is a bit modern and here I am subscribing to the more inclusive sense of the word hermeneutics.

Hermeneutics is a well-developed discipline in antiquity. For example, rabbinic hermeneutics distinguished *halakah* (norms derived from the sacred text), *haggadah* (often stories or other illustrations of the meaning of a sacred text) and their relationship to the sacred text *(midrash* attaches both kinds of material to the text, even interweaving them while *mishnah* does not). In addition, to enhance the understanding of Torah, there were the *targums* or translations of the sacred text into Aramaic that were given written form in the Christian period. Finally, there was *Talmud* that became the repository of these several kinds of writing.

Two names typically emerge within this tradition. The seven rules of Hillel are a compound of logic, analogy, context and consistency in the service of a common sense interpretation of the text. These seven rules seem to influence Tyconius and through him they pass to Augustine (for example in the *De Doctrina Christiana*, III, 30-37). I have found them in some detail in Irenaeus.[2]

The other prominent figure in this tradition is Philo. He is perhaps best known for his views on the complex and subtle sets of relationships between the literal and the allegorical.[3] Here we can see on the one hand the intellect ranging through related fields of application (the literal, metaphorical, moral, spiritual) and on the other the demand for a control of meaning in this very activity (as may be seen, for example, in Cicero's critique of allegory, *De Natura Deorum* I,15; II,18).

The classical tradition of rhetoric embraced the field of literary criticism providing it with a distinctive set of terms and relations. The strategies for refuting the claims of a myth or story are illustrated, for example, in Isocrates, Aelius Theon, Dio Chrysostom and Sextus Empiricus. Rhetorical and hermeneutical handbooks and manuals were a large part of the literary production of late antiquity. By and large, these assembled the criteria for literary probability in order to distinguish what is probable from what is true or merely false. Among these criteria were consistency, decorum (as excluding what is unbecoming), harmony and avoiding the absurd. There were other, more glamorous, examples of hermeneutics in the form, for example, of gematria in which a series of mystical relations are established between different things in accordance with the numerical value of the letters that spell out a particular word. Perhaps the most famous example of gematria is expressed in Rev 13:18 which speaks of a second beast, arising from the earth, whose name equals a number: "This calls for wisdom: let anyone with understanding calculate the number of the beast, for it is the number of a person. Its number is six hundred sixty-six." Reconstructing the name of the beast has proven elusive, but the common view is that the name is "Neron Caesar" which, in Hebrew gematria, equals 666. Perhaps because of its apparent biblical warrant, gematria is used favorably in the *Letter of Barnabas*, 9, in Clement of Alexandria (*Stromata* 6,11) and in Irenaeus (*Adversus Haereses* V, 30, 1). In antiquity, Scripture was understood under these various headings of hermeneutics. The issue is always meaning and the evidence adduced to support that meaning.

This state of affairs remains intact until the Enlightenment though certain relevant medieval developments are here postponed.[4] Now the tools and theories for investigating the past are unprecedented. Exegesis is the science that approaches a text with the question: 'What did this text likely mean for the author or for the listeners?' The tools to answer that question constitute the historical-critical method.

This method is in fact a collection of various critical disciplines, among them, literary criticism, textual, form, source and redaction criticism. Nowadays, it has been extended to embrace, for example, structuralism, deconstructionism, semiotics, narrative theory, Reader-Response theory. Here too should be added forms of Marxist, feminist and psychoanalytical hermeneutics. It should be said as well that such methods are entirely proper to a modern study of any text, including the sacred text. However, unhappily for this latter point, certain attitudes congregated round this scientific method. Among these, we can identify the view that religious and theological tradition must be grounded in historical criticism, that present experiences and events constitute criteria for establishing the probability of experiences and events said to have taken place in the past, and that all historical phenomena are interrelated as cause and effect. Such attitudes are likely to short-circuit one's approach to Scripture for which the claim is made that it is **norma normans non normata** – the normative textual witness to the Word of God in the Holy Spirit.

In the last century, this new criticism as applied to Scripture generated the now famous "quest of the historical Jesus." By turns, this movement separated out the Jesus of History from the dogmatic layers of the Christ of Faith. In this process, its various practitioners concurred in dismissing supernatural witness and mythical material as unhistorical. In 1906, Albert Schweitzer summed up much of this activity in his book *The Quest of the Historical Jesus*. He concluded that the gospels do not yield data for a historical life or historical biography of Jesus. In fact, he went on, Jesus' expectation of the final end of history was so intense as to undermine a modern search for the historical data on which to build a 'Life of Jesus.' Presumably Jesus did not think anything would be around for history to record.

Bultmann welcomed these developments as focusing attention on the issue of faith in Christ. Faith is pure risk and is undermined when allied with the cryptic human effort to ascertain 'objectivity' in religious matters and, thus, to control Christ. Bultmann taught that Faith has no historical foundation beyond the 'thatness' of Jesus. Moreover, Christ is present as Savior now in the encounter with the preached Word. In that encounter, there is no room for objectified, historically grounded facts.

This view of the matter was perhaps not likely to persuade many and indeed, in 1959, J.M. Robinson published *The New Quest of the Historical Jesus*, in which he attempts to hold on to the value of historical Jesus research while yet avoiding a relapse into 'Life of Jesus' biographies. Pace Bultmann, the work found lines of continuity between the historical ministry of Jesus and the Church's kerygmatic doctrine.

The issues associated with historical-critical method come home to roost in connection with the Resurrection of Jesus. Is the Resurrection a historical event? If so, is it in principle accessible to historical-critical method as is any other historical event? If so, what place does Faith have since presumably it is not needed to affirm the Resurrection event? And, if Resurrection is not a historical event, what kind of reality is it? Is it purely private, subjective and 'personal'? Does it perhaps exist only in a realm of fiction and the imagination?

Before these questions can be answered, it is necessary that their terms and relations be grounded in an adequate cognitional theory answering the question, 'What am I doing when I know?' and going on to an adequate epistemology in answer to the question, 'Why is doing that knowing?' Such an approach will account for Christology from below and, in its account of transforming love, for Christology from above. It will ground the distinction though not the results between the New Testament as testimony or faith and the New Testament as evidence for critical understanding in the tradition of modern exegesis and historical-critical method. In doing this such an approach will ground the distinction between the Jesus of History and the Christ of Faith. It will go on to distinguish history as fact, as moral value, and as 'saving' fact/moral value.

The results, very broadly, will be twofold. First, we will achieve a focus on Scriptural research as attending to the faith of the ancient church that is already expressed within the New Testament itself and thus is integral to it. As "faith texts", they yield evidence of levels of composition that may be identified as historical, oral and redaction levels. But an adequate cognitional theory will establish the point that these levels demand a more subtle approach than that of dismantling the oral and redaction levels, like so much scaffolding, in favor of the purely historical. One consequence of this view will be to question the adequacy of the "onion" image for the distinction between the Jesus of History and the Christ of Faith. These Scripture texts are not modern, detached, objective, scientific monographs. Another consequence will be to situate properly the systematics of the doctrine of the Resurrection. This means we begin not with an idea of history that already says what can and cannot happen but with the truth of the Resurrection as the sacred text teaches it and then we proceed to the meaningfulness of the affirmation that one who was dead is raised to life. This task leads to the second result, namely, that an adequate cognitional theory will ground the exciting prospect of advancing our knowledge of the thought and language, the culture, of the Jesus of History.

On this view, the twofold focus, namely, the New Testament as testimony or faith and the New Testament as evidence for critical understanding, is essential to adequate biblical research. The focus itself is grounded in the appeal to an adequate cognitional theory and in fact it reflects the biblical data. There is no question here of special pleading on behalf of the sacred text. At bottom, we attend to the New Testament data on the side of the object and to inquiring intelligence on the side of the subject. Such a cognitional theory will ground a critique of naiveté in either its rationalistic (Schweitzer, for example) or in its fundamentalist form (by asking why the compound of attending to data, understanding it correctly and judging it to be true is called knowing and by asking what that process looks like). Bernard Lonergan[5] has called this development a Christological heuristic structure that allows us to see the need and scope for further development in answer to the question 'Who do you say I am?'

This notion of a Christological heuristic structure seems a wholesome conclusion and a humane one. It is theological in the tradition that faith seeks understanding and not the other way round where one judges whether there is such a thing as faith. It is open and inquiring in its attention to the materials that constitute the thought, language and culture of the historical Jesus. In short, it fears nothing in the materials to which it attends. In this lies the dignity of our intellect that serves the dignity of our faith.

ESSAY TWO: JESUS AND JUDAISM

At the heart of Judaism lies "Torah". It embodies the Jewish encounter with the living God. Torah embraces an ensemble of experience, understanding and obligation. It has given Judaism its founding identity. Earlier, the sense of God had been a loose polytheism (the "elohim" gods) but there was a momentum toward the great breakthrough with Moses: "I appeared to Abraham, to Isaac, and to Jacob, as God Almighty, but by my name 'The Lord' I did not make myself known to them (Ex 6:3)." It is Adonai, the Lord, the One, the Only God, the Ineffable (YHWH), who is thus revealed unequivocally as God. Moses/Torah enshrines this experience of Revelation which contained the invitation and the means to be holy as the Lord is holy: "You shall be holy to me; for I the Lord am holy, and I have separated you from the other peoples to be mine (Lev 20:26)." Thus does Torah lie at the heart of Judaism. It is its soul. So central is the "Torah" experience that great care must be taken to protect its integrity. This solicitude was historically expressed in the concern to preserve its textual integrity and to assure the literal observance of Torah. This last point was often expressed as maintaining the "fence" around Torah. This fence was composed of a number of statutes, laws and commands and their observance helped to preserve the heart of Torah contained in the *Shema Israel*: "Hear, O Israel: The Lord Our God, the Lord is One (Dt 6:4)." This notion of Torah together with its fence was of fundamental and thorough importance since God was to be found there.

By the first century before Christ, a group appears called the Hakamim (the "Wise of Old"). We should perhaps think of them as predecessors to rabbinic Judaism. Their connection to Pharisaism is less clear. The Hakamim were devoted to preserving Torah. This meant that the Hakamim distanced themselves from the prophetic tradition. Their view seems to have been that, due to the sins of the nation, Israel's great prophetic tradition was over and done. Moreover, certain forms of prophecy were too charismatic or uncontrollable and therefore did not enjoy the same weight as the legal rulings of a rabbinic majority (the halakah). The halakah tradition is the fruit of Hakamim piety because it established the "boundary" conditions for faithfulness to Torah. This halakah tradition is the locus of authority over any single prophet at the risk of death. This appears to be very relevant to the appearance of Jesus and it makes Christology unavoidable.

So it is that Jesus appears increasingly as an alternative to the authority of the Hakamim boundary: He was asked, " 'By what authority are you doing these things? Who gave you this authority to do them?' (Mk 11:28)." Clearly, such questions demand some account of who Jesus is and of his relationship with the God of Israel. By and large, the gospels observe Jesus making his way toward Jerusalem, the center of the nation's life, of its emotions, decisions and authority. The fundamental insight the gospels present is that Jesus, who is very human, manifests God in the world, that Jesus is the visible effect of God in the world. This insight is distributed across his teachings and his miracles and these give rise to the issue of his authority in the land since the halakah tradition takes precedence over any single prophet. And Jesus understood himself as more than a prophet: "Why does this fellow speak in this way? It is blasphemy! Who can forgive sins but God alone (Mk 2:7)?"

This growing tension between Jesus and the Hakamim boundary tradition is dramatically expressed in his appearance before the Sanhedrin. The relevant context is Dt 17:8-13:

> "If a judicial decision is too difficult for you to make between one kind of bloodshed and another, one kind of legal right and another, or one kind of assault and another – any such matters of dispute in your towns – then you shall immediately go up to the place that the Lord your God will choose, where you shall consult with the levitical priests **and the judge who is in office in those days;** they shall announce to you the decision in the case. Carry out exactly the decision that they announce to you from the place that the Lord will choose, diligently observing everything they instruct you. You must carry out fully the law

that they interpret for you or the ruling that they announce to you; do not turn aside from the decision that they announce to you, either to the right or to the left. **As for anyone who presumes to disobey the priest appointed to minister there to the Lord your God, or the judge, that person shall die.** So you shall purge the evil from Israel. All the people will hear and be afraid, and will not act presumptuously again."

In the trial scene, it is the High Priest who is **the judge who is in office in those days**. Josephus expressly identified the High Priest as the Deuteronomic judge (*Antiquities*,iv,218) as did Philo before him (*De Specialibus Legibus,*iv,190). And if, by his silence, Jesus does not accept the authority of the High Priest to authenticate his teaching, then Jesus is appealing to someone else. He is appealing to the "Son of Man."

The phrase "Son of Man" has generated a great deal of scholarship.[6] Here I would like to trace some relevant developments of the phrase. Son of Man was recognized as associated with human frailty as subject to death. This is the principal view of the phrase taken by the Old Testament and it envisions Adam's penalty of death ("ben Adam" in Hebrew may also mean "Son of Man"): "By the sweat of your face you shall eat bread until you return to the ground, for out of it you were taken; you are dust and to dust you shall return (Gen 3:19)." The Letter to the Hebrews combines this notion of "man born to die" with a divine vindication of him. Referring to Psalm 8, the text reads:

> " 'What are human beings that you are mindful of them, or mortals, that you care for them? You have made them for a little while lower than the angels; you have crowned them with glory and honor, subjecting all things under their feet.' Now in subjecting all things to them, God left nothing outside their control. As it is, we do not yet see everything in subjection to them, **but we do see Jesus, who for a little while was made lower than the angels, now crowned with glory and honor because of the suffering of death, so that by the grace of God he might taste death for everyone** (Heb 2:6-9)."

This combination of the one liable to death yet vindicated by God is found in Mk 10:45: "For the Son of Man came not to be served but to serve, and to give his life as a ransom for many." These references express the self-consciousness of Jesus in his relationship to God. This relationship was characterized by faith and not by observance of the (rabbinic) fence around Torah.

What faith does Jesus possess? Increasingly Scripture uses the term faith not only as the adequate expression for the way the chosen people related to God but even more to express God's faithfulness toward his people which the faith of the people was invited to imitate. Jesus embodies this twofold fullness of faith. The law and the prophets had spoken about him (Jn 5:46; Lk 24:44) and with him they conversed on the Mount of the Transfiguration (Mt 17:3). He "is the one on the basis of whom every Old Testament believer has lived (Heb 11)."[7] Inasmuch as the New Testament fulfills the Old, to that extent it requires of Jesus and of all believers the faithfulness and obedience of faith. But equally, when faith is directed to the truth of the kerygma, then Christ, as the content of the kerygma, stands over faith.

The New Testament does not use the term faith to express Jesus' basic attitude as Son of Man toward God. Instead it is drawn to a different series of terms, for example, fidelity, trust, preferring the Father before all, persevering in this attitude, handing everything over to the Father including even knowledge of the end (Mk 13:32). In turn, this attitude is the source of Jesus' power displayed in his miracles and which, as the attitude of faith, he imparts to his disciples. This attitude of faith John the Evangelist calls love.

He taught this whole attitude of faith publicly and in the Temple precincts. In his arraignment before the High Priest together with the Sanhedrin it was necessary to situate the authentic locus of authority – in the "judge who is in office in those days" or in the "Son of Man." In this confrontation, arranged to determine whether he belonged in the category described in Dt 17:8-13, Jesus appears to reject the final authority of that judge. As such he could be read as the contumacious rebel exactly envisioned in the Deuteronomic text, though not all were persuaded. One last effort to have him invoke the prophetic spirit for his authority likewise failed: "Some began to spit on him, to blindfold him, and to strike him, saying to him, 'Prophesy!" The guards also took him over and beat him (Mk 14:65)." So it was that death, the penalty prescribed by Deuteronomy, at the same time characterizes the figure of the "Son of Man." But the "Son of Man" tradition added the notion of God's vindication of his servant.

In the New Testament, this vindication is expressed in the apostolic experience of a Jesus who they knew was dead yet he was alive in the eucharist and in their experience of his bodily presence to them which filled them with a great fear. One very strong implication of associating "Son of Man" and "Resurrection from the dead" lies in the fact that the divine vindication is exactly ordered to one who is dead as liable to death. Thus, the phrase "Son of Man" anchors the notion of Resurrection against the psychologizing tendency that explains Resurrection away, for example, in terms of overwrought memory or eternal springtime or some other variant. The tradition speaks of a man, a real human being, who was literally dead and who now lives. Such a truth presents its own difficulties, but these should not be added to by importing views that do not square with the "Son of Man" tradition.

The gospel tradition of the Son of Man manifests as well the Christian understanding of God as Trinity. The Trinitarian relations of self-giving are expressed in the *kenosis* of the Son of God and provide the condition for the possibility of Creation itself. Contained in *kenosis* and creation are the suffering of the cross and the Trinitarian Eucharist of the Son. As long as life lasts, the meaning of our earthly life remains obscured and undecided. In death, however, through the divine judgment, one receives one's definitive orientation. For this reason, the Incarnation is itself ordered to the Passion and Death of Christ. God experiences our estranged and sinful human condition 'from within' in order to save it. The state of being dead of the Incarnate Word is not one situation among others in the life of Jesus – a brief interruption of a life resumed again at Easter. There is no common measure between the death of a human being, from which one cannot return, and 'resurrection'. But what is unique here is the affirmation that One has died for All. Obedience to the Father unites Christ's kenotic Incarnation with the fact that this *kenosis* is divinely willed by him who is the 'form of God.' His *kenosis* translates the eternal love of the Son for the ever-greater Father. In obedience the Son submits to the lead and mission of the Spirit. Thus, obedience constitutes the truth that Christ's existence, functionally and kenotically, is ordered to the cross that manifests Trinitarian love.

This essay has isolated the tradition of the "boundary" conditions of Torah over against the "Son of Man" tradition of the prophetic and postexilic writings. The drama of the confrontation between them constitutes an essential aspect of the Passion of Jesus as the gospels record it. On the view set out here, it is possible to understand what was at stake. This view also points ahead to St. Paul who saw matters pretty much as they are laid out here. It helps account for the sheer intensity with which Paul departs from pharisaism and the fence about Torah to embrace faith in the Son of Man unto salvation, grace and glory.

ESSAY THREE: PAUL

Who is Paul? In his own mind, he was an apostle:

> "Last of all, as to one untimely born, he {Christ} appeared also to me. For I am the least of the apostles, unfit to be called an apostle, because I persecuted the church of God. But by the grace of God I am what I am and his grace toward me was not in vain (1Cor 15:8-10)."

And again:

> "...for I am not at all inferior to these super-apostles, even though I am nothing (2Cor 12:11b)."

Yet Paul does not fit the criteria of an apostle as set down, for example, for the election that chose Matthias to replace Judas Iscariot:

> "So one of the men who have accompanied us during all the time that the Lord Jesus went in and out among us, beginning from the baptism of John until the day when he was taken up from us – one of these must become a witness with us to his resurrection (Acts 1:21-22)."

Paul did not accompany the others during all the time the Lord walked with them, but he had no doubt that he was a witness of the risen Lord. And what is one to make of the vision of St. John in Revelation that does not appear to square with Paul's self-understanding:

> "Then I saw a new heaven and a new earth ... And I saw the holy city, new Jerusalem, coming down out of heaven ... as

> a bride .... Then one of the seven angels ... said to me, 'Come, I will show you the bride, the wife of the Lamb.' ... It has the glory of God ... And the wall of the city has twelve foundations, and on them are the twelve names of the twelve apostles of the Lamb (Rev 21:1,2,9-14, condensed)."

The Seer of Patmos does not apparently count 13 apostles and this may point to an underlying ambiguity regarding Paul's apostolic claim.

In any event, Paul very nearly boasts of the independent cast of his mind. He withstands Peter to his face, accusing him of inconstancy in the matter of the Gentiles and the requirement of circumcision (Gal 2:11-14). More than to the "super" apostles, the largest share of the mystery of Christ falls to him to record and to preach. Luke and Mark are his companions and his deeds occupy the greater part of the Acts of the Apostles. He was martyred in Rome during the reign of Nero, perhaps sometime in 65. Paul had been under house arrest there (61-63). Nero (emperor from 54-68) was unspeakably brutal. Paul's death is part of a cataclysm of imperial fear and venality. The list of the dead is lengthy: Britannicus, the 14 year old son of the Emperor Claudius; Octavia, Nero's wife and daughter of Claudius; the emperor's own mother; then Burrus, the Prefect of the Praetorian Guard. When, in the year 65, the famous plot to kill Nero was uncovered, more deaths followed. Among them one counts Seneca the Younger and the poet Lucan.

Some have held the view that Paul has taken the simple preaching of a rural Palestinian itinerant preacher and corrupted it into a Hellenistic mystery religion of salvation. For others, Paul is the preacher of the pure gospel of "faith alone" against all works righteousness and thus the veritable founder of Protestant Christianity. Catholic "Paulinism" on the other hand has concentrated on the letters to the Corinthians with their clear assertion of Paul's authority over that church, an assertion almost Petrine in its ring. "So I write this ... while I am away ... so that when I come, I may not have to be severe in using the authority that the Lord has given me for building up and not for tearing down (2Cor 13:10)."

All this is curious, even humorous in its way, regarding one who began his career as a Pharisee of the school of Gamaliel, the foremost Pharisee of the time. What accounts for the change Paul experienced and which is vividly expressed in his repudiation of the Pharisaic view of Torah? For that, we must go out along the road leading from Jerusalem to Damascus.

The Acts of the Apostles describes Paul's conversion experience (between 32 and 34A.D.) in three variants. It was in fact a mystical experience. It was characterized by an intensity experienced by him as unmediated and such an "unmediated" experience lies at the heart of mystical experience. He sensed that he had been overtaken by the holy. Sometime later, Paul had a similar experience:

> "I know a person (Paul speaks here indirectly of himself) in Christ who fourteen years ago was caught up to the third heaven—whether in the body or out of the body I do not know; God knows. And I know that such a person – whether in the body or out of the body I do not know; God knows – was caught up into Paradise and heard things that are not to be told, that no mortal is permitted to repeat (2Cor 12:2-4)."

With this description, Paul shares a world in common with both the Hekhaloth books of mystical revelations and with strands of Jewish Gnosticism. Some apocalyptic motifs speak of three heavens, as here, others of seven. Some Gnostic traditions speak of eight heavens (the Ogdoad). These differences appear to be variations on a common theme of mystical ascent.

One of these traditions of Jewish mysticism is *Merkabah* mysticism. It seems likely that Paul was praying as a Merkabah initiate while on the road to Damascus. The Hebrew word *Merkabah* refers to the war-chariot with its fiery wheels as depicted in the first chapter of Ezekiel. By imagining this vision, the initiate ascends through the seven heavens. There are angelic ranks, demons and magical formulae along the way. The sixth heaven is especially dangerous as the Talmudic story of the Four who entered Paradise relates. In the seventh heaven, the *Merkabah* initiate beholds in a vision the One who sits upon the throne:

> "And above the dome over their heads (of the four living creatures) there was something like a throne, in appearance like sapphire; and seated above the likeness of a throne was something that seemed like a human form (Ezek 1:26)."

Sometimes this likeness of a human form is called the divine *dynamis*, the power or the Glory of God ("… suddenly a light from heaven flashed around him, Acts 9:3"). This tradition of *Merkabah* mysticism clarifies and yields a deeper grasp of Paul's conversion experience. In place of this likeness of a human form, Paul heard the likeness of Jesus' human voice saying to him in Hebrew, 'Saul, Saul, why are you persecuting me?' …. "I am Jesus … (Acts 26:14-15)." The encounter is public. The others heard the voice, but saw no one (Acts 9:7) or else saw the light, but heard nothing (Acts 22:9) or with Paul all fell to the ground at the same time (Acts 26:14). The encounter is with the glory of Christ yet the brief conversation achieves a striking intimacy: "Saul, Saul…I am Jesus." Paul is blinded and he enters Damascus like a blind beggar. On the strength of this experience, Paul underwent his now famous conversion and he set to writing and preaching the mystery of Christ as suffering, crucified and raised up. I do not think this devotion to the person of Christ is to be found in quite the same way anywhere else in the New Testament. As the Lord said to Ananias, "I myself will show him how much he **must** suffer for the sake of my name (Acts 9:16)." This suffering for the sake of Jesus' name constituted Paul's credentials as an apostle: "May I never boast of anything except the cross of our Lord Jesus Christ…(Gal l6: 14)." Indeed Paul received this suffering in his own body: "for I carry the marks of Jesus branded on my body (Gal 6:17)." His suffering is bitterly real. He is treated like a death-row inmate (1Cor 4:9), as "the rubbish of the world, the dregs of all things (1Cor 4:13)." Everyone deserted him at his first trial (2Tim 4:16). Indeed, the more he loved the Church, the less he was loved by her (2Cor 12:15). Over and over one sees this sustained twofold focus on the apostle and the man, the office and the suffering, the preacher and the man of prayer. As a New Testament portrait it is utterly unique.[8]

Paul has broken through to existence "in Christ." Jesus crucified has crossed over to sinners and established the reconciliation between God and us and the new unity of love of God and love of each other:

> "For he is our peace; in his flesh he has made both groups into one and has broken down the dividing wall, that is, the hostility between us. He has abolished the law with its commandments and ordinances, that he might create in himself one new humanity (*hena kainon anthropon*) in place of the two, thus

> making peace, and might reconcile both groups to God in one body through the cross, thus putting to death that hostility through it (Eph 2:14-16)."

Christ crucified has abolished in his flesh the law of commandments and ordinances. This deeply moving theme of the passage from Torah to Gospel is laid out in the letter to the Romans. Law and commandments could only point out sin, but could not prevent it. Only faith in Christ produced justification. Observing the law was of no help. The unity achieved in Christ ("God is faithful; by him you were called into the fellowship of his Son, Jesus Christ our Lord," 1Cor 1:9") is sometimes expressed in terms of the eucharist: "The cup of blessing … is it not a sharing in the blood of Christ? The bread … is it not a sharing in the body of Christ (1Cor 10:16)?" Sometimes it is expressed in terms of the Holy Spirit: "If then there is any encouragement in Christ, any consolation from love, any sharing in the Spirit, any compassion and sympathy, make my joy complete: be of the same mind…(Phil 2:1-2)." This unity in Christ is also described in terms of the analogy of the body and its parts. It extends to the sharing of material and spiritual goods. It even extends to the extraordinary practice, in Corinth at least, of being baptized on behalf of the dead: "Otherwise, what will those people do who receive baptism on behalf of the dead? If the dead are not raised at all, why are people baptized on their behalf (1Cor 15:29)?" So far from being a 'private' affair, baptism affects even the dead by establishing a unity with them. The doctrine of the Communion of Saints is relevant here. Even our bodiliness expresses the union of persons in nuptial sacramentality. All these perspectives appear to be contained in the expression of life and unity "in Christ." As Paul writes by way of concluding the Corinthian correspondence, "Do you not realize that Jesus Christ is in you (2Cor 13:5)?"

On the way to Damascus, Paul encountered the grace of Christ crucified. His conversion to Jesus was instant and thorough. It took hold of him at the level of intellectual and moral conversion. No one knew quite what to make of him or quite what to do with him. In a flash of light, Paul appears to have seen the whole mystery of glory. It is extraordinary that one who approved of the killing of Stephen (Acts 8: 1) and who breathed threats and murder (Acts 9:1) against the disciples of the Lord should himself become a disciple and indeed an apostle.

With limpid purity and bursting exuberance Paul contemplated the One who asked "Who do you say I am?"

ESSAY FOUR

THE CHURCH AND ISRAEL

Within the theme of Jesus and Judaism there lies the form of the Church and of Israel. As the People of God, the Church is composed of Jews and Gentiles:

> "...remember that at one time you Gentiles by birth ... were at that time without Christ, being aliens from the commonwealth of Israel, and strangers to the covenants of promise, having no hope and without God in the world. But now in Christ Jesus you who once were far off have been brought near by the blood of Christ. For he is our peace; in his flesh he has made both groups into one and has broken down the dividing wall, that is, the hostility between us....that he might create in himself one new humanity in place of the two, thus making peace, and might reconcile both groups to God in one body through the cross... (Eph 2:11-16)."

But it is also the deeply moving view of St. Paul (Rom 11) that the Church is born at the point where Israel has said "No" to Jesus as the Christ. As the Fourth Gospel observes: "His own received him not (Jn 1:11)." Thus does tragedy lie at the origins of the Church. And it will seem to many that this tragedy has cast a long, dark shadow down the length of our common history. In any case, the form of the Church is shaped by Israel's "No."

What is this shape of the Church? It is made up of the continued historical existence of Israel and the Church. It is a vivid, even a daily reminder of the mercy of God according to the meditation of St. Paul in Rom 9-11. What influence, Paul wonders, would Israel's "Yes" have had on the form of the Church? That is a way of speaking of the End when God shall be all in all. For the moment, however, let us observe that, for Paul, there is also an Israel that does receive Jesus as the Christ. It is the 'remnant' Israel of which the prophets have spoken. It is this remnant that, together with the Gentiles, makes up the Church as the People of God, the New Israel.

The remnant Israel has entered the Church: "Peace and mercy…be upon the Israel of God (Gal 6:16)." As such, Israel brings into the Church the notions of election in pure grace, redemption from sin, faith in God, faithfulness to God's will, the great commandment, the presence of God in the whole people (which will characterize the whole Church as the Body of Christ), the life of priestly service and atonement. Israel is a stranger among the nations as the place where God dwells in holiness. "Salvation is from the Jews (Jn 4:22)." So, one may add, is the idea of the Church as a community or a society.

The "other" Israel stumbles and falls over the cornerstone that is Christ (Eph 2:20). Paul especially feels the sadness. He could almost wish to be himself accursed and cut off from Christ for the sake of his brethren, his kin by race (Rom 9:3). Yet he sees that the "hardening" of Israel (Rom 11:7) manifests the extension of God's mercy toward the Gentiles. So it is that history is now the story of "two Israels": the new Israel and the old, the Church and the Synagogue. The existence of two Israels indicates that history is fundamentally the story of divine mercy.

Israel is founded in the election of Abraham. Israel is a people of God and of the land, of blood and race, of obedience to the covenant. Circumcision testifies to it (Gen 17:9-14). But Abraham is also father in faith and his journey, which begins as obedience to a call of God, is directed toward a faithfulness which anticipates in its embrace both law and prophecy. It is this faithfulness that constitutes the "true" Israel, the remnant. It is important then to keep in view both Israel as an ethnic people and Israel as a faithful (remnant) people. This twofold constitution points to Christ who is both a Jew and the faithful one. It also expresses Israel's deepest self-understanding, that is, the truth that God has chosen Israel from among all other nations. This fact determines its way of life (ethos) and its goal in the Messianic end-time (a theology of history). This election to faith likewise serves as a standard against which Israel is repeatedly called to conversion. There is always the tendency to collapse Torah into legalism and true worship into ritual sacrifice, even idolatry. There is likewise ever the tendency to confuse divine wisdom with the great wisdom traditions of court, politics and diplomacy. The issue of faithfulness accounts for the divine wrath and its threat to reject Israel (for example, Hos 11:5-7) and to curse him (Dt 28:15-19). The election to faith, faithfulness as the fruit of conversion, complete dependence on God – these extend to the time of the gospels. In a word, election means that God chooses the poor and humble. Israel was once so (Dt 7:7). With the gospels, the gentiles too are now among the foolish and weak "that no one may boast in the presence of God (1Cor 1:27ff)."

Jesus of Nazareth, "the Christ, the Son of the living God", is the great stumbling stone. Yet even here God's mercy is seen as directed toward the Gentiles: "I tell you, many will come from east and west and will eat with Abraham and Isaac and Jacob in the kingdom of heaven, while the heirs of the kingdom will be thrown into the outer darkness… (Mt 8:11-12)." The parables of vine and vineyard go to make the same point. Yet Nathanael is a true Israelite (the remnant or receiving Israel) who acknowledges Jesus as King of Israel (Jn 1: 47,49). In all this, Israel is left behind but not rejected: "I ask, then, has God rejected his people? By no means (Rom 11:1)!" But Israel failed to obtain what it sought (Rom 11:7). Put differently: "See, your house is left to you, desolate. For I tell you, you will not see me again, until you say, 'Blessed is the one who comes in the name of the Lord (Mt 23:38-39)."

Indeed, the governing relationship between the old Israel and the new appears to be drawn theologically from the encounter between Abraham and Melchizedek in whose high priesthood Jesus shares:

> "This 'King Melchizedek of Salem, priest of the Most High God, met Abraham as he was returning from defeating the kings and blessed him'; and to him Abraham apportioned 'one-tenth of everything.' His name…means 'king of righteousness'; next he is also king of Salem, that is, 'king of peace.' Without father, without mother, without genealogy, having neither beginning of

> days nor end of life, but resembling the Son of God he remains a priest for ever (Heb 7:1-3; and see Gen 14:17-20)."

Abraham's call to be the father in faith of Jew and Gentile follows his mysterious meeting here with Christ who is symbolized in Melchizedek: "Your ancestor Abraham rejoiced that he would see my day; he saw it and was glad (Jn 8:56)." Abraham and all his seed (especially Levi in whom the Old Testament priesthood is contained) bow before Melchizedek who resembles the Son of God. Put differently, Church and Synagogue spring from the same parent, that is, the sacrificial cult of the Temple. When the Romans destroyed it in 70A.D., the two siblings tended to grow apart. In a hundred years the separation was more or less complete.

As it happens, the essential difference between the old Israel and the new has to do with the Church's sense of mission. It is the difference between an ethnic community and a community of those who are born again of water and the Spirit (Jn 3:3). This is an important point, notwithstanding the clear universalizing tendencies throughout Israel's history. The Risen Christ has sent the Church in these last days to continue His own mission. Thus is she catholic, engaging distance, time, culture, humanity, the creation. To this end, He has equipped her with His Spirit who makes us the body and therefore the bride of Christ in the sacraments and brings forth vocations and mission, charisms and talents: "until all of us come to the unity of the faith and of the knowledge of the Son of God, to maturity, to the measure of the full stature of Christ… speaking the truth in love, we must grow up in every way into him who is the head, into Christ … (Eph 4:13,15)."

Increasingly in the New Testament the Christian mission is well established with its invitation to believe in Jesus Christ and his gospcl:

> "{Jesus Christ} is the image of the invisible God, the first-born of all creation; for in him… all things have been created … and for him. He himself is before all things, and in him all things hold together. He is the head of the body, the church; he is the beginning, the first-born from the dead, so that he might come to have first place in everything. For in him all the fullness of God was pleased to dwell, and through him God was pleased to reconcile to himself all things, whether on earth or in heaven, by

> making peace through the blood of his cross. And you who once were estranged and hostile in mind, doing evil deeds, he has now reconciled in his fleshly body through his death, so as to present you holy … before him …. It is he whom we proclaim, warning everyone and teaching everyone in all wisdom, so that we may present everyone mature in Christ (Col 1:15-21)."

This is testimony indeed to Jesus Christ as the Lord of Glory. A prevailing image and theme in these verses is his body which we are. His crucified body is the place of our reconciliation. His risen body attests to his pre-eminence in all and before all. Closely related to the Church as the Body of Christ is the image of the Church as the Bride of Christ:

> "For the husband is the head of the wife just as Christ is the head of the church, the body of which he is the Savior …. Husbands, love your wives, just as Christ loved the church and gave himself up for her … to make her holy by cleansing her with the washing of water by the word, so as to present the church to himself in splendor, without a spot or wrinkle … holy and without blemish. In the same way, husbands should love their wives as they do their own bodies …. For no one ever hates his own body, but he nourishes and tenderly cares for it, just as Christ does for the church, because we are members of his body. For this reason a man will leave his father and mother and be joined to his wife and the two shall become one flesh. This mystery … I am applying … to Christ and the church (Eph 5: 23-32)."

Here St. Paul speaks of the church as the bride of Christ and this image mediates both the image of the church as his body and that of the church as the People of God. The image of the bride allows one to see the proper distance between the church and Christ, while at the same time personifying the whole people of God in intimacy with Christ. In doing this, the image of bride disallows both a positivist ecclesiology and the view that ecclesiology is in fact a branch of sociology. Together the images of body and people, mediated in the image of bride, gather together sexuality, marriage, eucharist, priesthood and

> community: "Come, I will show you the Bride, the wife of the Lamb (Rev 21:9)." And the Seer of Patmos was shown the Jerusalem above "who is free and she is our mother (Gal 4: 26)."

The bride originates in the *sacrum commercium*, the holy exchange whose origin is the self-renunciation of Christ on the cross. His self-renunciation becomes her form of life, the life of the one who loved us "to the end (Jn 13:1)." The crucified Lord exchanges our sinfulness for his glory, our death for his life. Out of love, Christ sinks into powerlessness and desperation. The Father rejects him as the sin of the world. The Church emerges from this extraordinary circumstance in which absolute love appears under the form of sin. This is already Easter grace making splendid the cross of Christ that brings us to birth and life by the poverty of his selflessness, a Final Eve from the side of the Last Adam who thus contains the church within himself. In other words, the solidarity of Christ with us, his bride, even extends to the attitude and consequences of our sinfulness: "For we do not have a high priest who is unable to sympathize with our weaknesses, but we have one who in every respect has been tested as we are, yet without sin (Heb 4:15)."

We see then that the image of bride personifies the people of God in terms of unity and intimacy with God. The image of Mary serves a similar function. She appears in the gospels as already a consequence of Christ's "Yes" to the world. That "Yes" is mediated through her (responding) yes to be mother of the Messiah. She is united with Christ in the obedience of their common "Yes" to the Father. Christ's "Yes" makes possible a responding "Yes" – first in Mary and then in many brothers and sisters who together are the Church. Mary personifies the mediating function of the Church which is thus constituted by Christ's "Yes" and creation's responding "Yes" in the form of obedience and renunciation. The Church is this place of encounter precisely established by God, the bride's responding "Yes" to her spouse's initiating "Yes."[9]

We have been dealing with the nature of the Church in Balthasar's writings and so far the basic terms and relations have been drawn from St. Paul, especially from the letter to the Ephesians, and from the letter to the Hebrews. One might also expect that Balthasar would draw substantially on St. John the Evangelist and in fact that is the case. For one thing, Balthasar distinguishes the two of them. Unlike Paul, the Lord had no need to overpower John to win his allegiance. From the moment John saw the Lord and heard his voice,[10] John was drawn out of himself and into the pure seeing, hearing and touching of the love that was revealed to him: "We declare to you what was from the beginning, what we have heard, what we have seen with our eyes, what we have looked at and touched with our hands, concerning the word of life… .what we have seen and heard so that you also may have fellowship with us … (1Jn 1:1,3)." When John emerged from this experience to announce what he had seen and heard, he could only proclaim the wonder of the Lord's love. Whereas Paul's individuality projected itself precisely for the sake of his mission and drew all eyes to itself ("Brethren, be imitators of me, Phil 3:17."), John's individuality was extinguished, its outline erased. His whole being became transparent so that the one light of Christ might shine through it.

On the terms of the Fourth Gospel then Balthasar has built into the foundation of his ecclesiology a meditation on the "three Marys" — Mary of Bethany, Mary Magdalene and Mary, the Mother of the Lord. This meditation draws out the significance of the origin of the Church at the cross of Christ, a central motif of that ecclesiology. Mary of Bethany is sister to Martha and Lazarus. St. John records that Mary anointed Jesus' feet with a costly perfume of pure nard in token of his imminent death and burial (Jn 12:1-8). Earlier, she had "sat at the Lord's feet and listened to what he was saying (Lk 10:39)." Balthasar identifies Mary as the first person in the gospels to say 'yes' to the kind of Messiah Jesus understands himself to be. By bitter contrast, Peter persists in telling the Lord how he should be Messiah (e.g., Mt 16:21-23). Mary accepts that in Jesus, God's love for us is crucified. Unlike Judas, her contemplative love of God does not calculate love so as to make it useful. She does not consider that the perfume could have been sold and the return (nearly a year's wages for a laborer) given to the poor (Jn 12:5). In this, Mary sets no limits and makes no demands on God. She renounces any effort to manipulate Jesus. Her posture is pure openness to the cross of Christ. That is why Jesus says of her "Mary has chosen the better part" (Lk 10:42) in listening to Jesus and it "will not be taken away from her."

The "second" Mary is Magdalene. She stands at the foot of the cross when all the men have fled. It was perhaps here that she learned how much it cost Christ to deliver her from seven devils (Mk 16:9) to a new freedom and existence. By God's mercy, she represents sinners everywhere, redeemed by the cross. Her vigil at the cross is really quite useless in that she can do nothing for him. Even in death, the men remove the body and place it in the lap of Christ's mother. Magdalene, however, maintains her sense of keeping vigil: "Mary Magdalene and the other Mary were there, sitting opposite the tomb (Mt 27:61)." Between her and the dead Christ there is placed a great stone boulder. In this devastation, she is the first witness of the Resurrection. Speaking her name, "Mary!", Christ drives from her the darkness of suffering and death. He floods her soul with the whole light of his Resurrection. Being a witness, Mary is also given a mission – she cannot have Christ on her terms: "Do not hold on to me....go to my brothers (Jn 20:17)" and tell them I go to the Father. Mary obeys. She "went and announced to the disciples, 'I have seen the Lord'; and she told them that he had said these things to her (v. 18)." Here the Church's witness to the Resurrection begins. It begins with Mary who is not a legitimate witness in Jewish law and whose witness is dismissed even by the apostles – her words "seemed to them an idle tale, and they did not believe … (Lk 24:12)." The Risen Christ actually scolds them for their unbelief: "Later, he appeared to the eleven themselves as they were sitting at the table; and he upbraided them for their lack of faith and stubbornness, because they had not believed those who saw him after he had risen (Mk 16:14)."

Finally, there is the "third" Mary, the Mother of the Lord. She is listed first among those at the foot of the cross: "Meanwhile, standing near the cross of Jesus were his mother …. When Jesus saw his mother and the disciple whom he loved standing beside her, he said to his mother, 'Woman, here is your son.' Then he said to the disciple, 'Here is your mother.' And from that hour the disciple took her into his own home (Jn 19:25-27)." At the foot of the cross, Mary is silent. She is 'given away' to John. She is not asked about these arrangements whereby she becomes mother to John and he a son to her. Her agreement is presupposed by the Lord as has been the case since the Annunciation itself. At that time, she was asked once and once only for her assent, her "fiat", to the office of mother of the messiah. Ever after, she is led in faith to be a disciple of her son. Her particular role, however, at the foot of the cross is to let Jesus go, abandoning him to the Father.

This theology of the three Marys discloses basic elements of Balthasar's ecclesiology in a biblical and accessible way. These elements may be listed as contemplation, witness and mission. These terms express the fact that one is in agreement (the Johannine 'indifference') with the sacrifice of the crucified Lord and that this agreement is fundamentally feminine.[11] On this basis one can work out Balthasar's understanding of the Church in a coherent fashion.

One notes finally how this ecclesiology differs from other meditations on the nature of the Church such as those broadly inspired by liberation theology with its concern to evangelize unjust economic and social structures or those inspired by sociology, by feminism with its critique of hierarchy, or indeed by systems analysis.[12] By comparison Balthasar may seem insufficiently critical and this is an important point. It can be said, for example, that his understanding of the Church leans toward *Lumen Gentium* rather than toward *Gaudium et Spes* with its discussion of the economic and political realms. Yet Balthasar has advanced an ecclesiology that is deeply biblical and Catholic. It never loses sight of the fact that in all matters the Church refers to Christ. Despite its real limitations I contend that it is a more rounded and complete achievement than the understandings of the Church that must nevertheless supplement it.

PART II

ESSAY FIVE: THE NOTION OF "CLASSICAL" OR "PATRISTIC" CHRISTOLOGY

The term 'classicism' has drawn to itself a number of conceits and prejudices. For example, the Renaissance was seen as an encounter with classical antiquity of such a scope as to bring about a 'rebirth' of European culture. In this view, the classical humanism of the Renaissance seemed to 'jump over' the 'middle' period (the medieval period) that, in some sense, it brought to an end. There are those who see in this the note of victory, of vanquishing an extended dark age, dim and dreary, a too long interval stretching from Plutarch to Petrarch. Thus, medieval culture is sacrificed on the altar of a Renaissance classicism, our true *fons et origo.* Or again, there is the memorable view of T.S. Eliot who argued the enduring relevance of classicism precisely in its preservation of what is common and shared in the West over centuries. This is a fitting reminder at a time of tremendous specialization in education and the professions. Perhaps too classicism serves as an antidote to the various tyrannies of the present. It is even possible to become quite sentimental about the classical world, to sink into a kind of genteel antiquarianism in the spirit of Mr. Chips turned out in tweeds, with afternoon tea, weekend rugby and a dead poets' society.

On the other hand, one may find all this classical venerability merely tiresome and prefer to take one's stand alongside Francis Bacon. One then deplores the pre-modern, pre-critical and pre-scientific nature of the intellectual life of antiquity. Similarly, the stage was set for the *querelle des anciens et des modernes* in the literary world of the *Grand Siecle* of Louis XIV. This "*querelle*" pitted classical literary normativity against the national literature and language of France that was growing in self-confidence and creative impulse. But the "*querelle*" came to symbolize something larger, the struggle between classicism and historicity.

At first, the wave of the future seemed set against classicism in favor of modernity. More recently, however, the critical importance of antiquity has once again been championed, for example, by Martin Heidegger in metaphysics, by Leo Strauss in his return to the fair and humane classical account of political order and natural law and by Eric Voegelin in his work on classical reason. At the very beginning of *Being and Time*, Heidegger remarks on the necessity, the structure and the priority of the question of Being. His retrieval of the spirit of wonder with which Greek thought encountered the question of Being is of the greatest importance. Being is the most universal concept yet the darkest of all concepts. For Being is indefinable. It cannot be considered as an 'entity,' understood as something that is. Yet the indefinability of Being does not eliminate the question of its meaning. This project of rethinking Being is intensively Greek and presocratic. It stands apart from Kant, Hegel, Phenomenology, even Plato in the direction of the Aegean dawn and the archaic age. Here we seem to sense something pure and uncontaminated. Perhaps our present ecological crisis moves us to deplore the loss of an ancient connection with Being, Nature, Creation in which there may lie answers to our present problems. In *Natural Right and History*, Leo Strauss championed the classical tradition of natural right that he understood to be connected to a teleological view of the cosmos. Everything in nature has a natural end and a natural destiny and this fact shapes rational moral awareness. Without some such grounding the alternative is an unqualified relativism and historicism from which the eternal and the divine is excluded. The challenge is for reason or philosophy to rediscover "nature" as foundational and authoritative. Indeed, once discovered, nature sets the standard, namely, that the good is more fundamental than the pleasant, knowledge more fundamental than opinion and that the human being is by nature a social being.

Voegelin is very much in this vein. His retrieval of antiquity affirms a human nature that is structured and therefore limited in terms of its perfectibility. Philosophy wishes to advance from opinion to knowledge. Society is human existence writ large and that existence is an erotic tension with its divine ground. These perspectives indicate that human existence is disturbed by the question of the ground and seeks to understand this relationship. In this unrest, the reality of divine-human participation (*metalepsis*) becomes luminous as the foundational concern of philosophy, disclosing the life of reason as constitutive of human nature. Freedom appears in the human commitment to the life of reason. One recognizes the classical worldview in these twentieth century thinkers.[13]

Still the issues raised by the modern appeal to human historicity will not go away. Indeed, they are too important to postpone any longer and some effort must now be made to sort out some directions. Classicism studied "nature" as the domain of science and metaphysics. This meant that the intellectual life studied what is necessary, universal and eternal. It understood knowledge as certainty about unchanging truths. This also meant the study of a "human nature" which was constant for all people, places and times. Classicism understood human culture as normatively expressed in Greece and, perhaps, also in Rome. In any case, the standards, the "norms", were achieved in the past and the task of the present and future is to imitate or otherwise preserve this achievement. Wisdom lay in the past too. On this view, creativity and innovation are not much valued.

The alternative to such classicism is an appeal to human historicity. What is the difference? Human historicity means that human living is informed by meanings, that meanings are the products of intelligence, that intelligence develops cumulatively over time and that this cumulative development differs in different histories. On this view, the classical world is itself one (particularly splendid) example of such cumulative development even as it failed to see that such development is quite open and ongoing. This view displaces culture as normative in favor of a view of culture as empirical. Thus culture is defined as a set of meanings and values that inform a common way of life. Such a definition underscores the importance of the human understanding of the human. Or, what comes to the same thing, human culture is human self-expression by means of acts of meaning that are historically conditioned.

It is important to rehearse for one's self the significance of this shift from a classicist to a historicist foundation. When the shift is negotiated, one still enjoys and learns from antiquity, but one does not make its self-understanding one's own. Now one asks "what is going forward in the passage from the pre-modern world to modernity?" though that is a very large question indeed. It opens onto a series of dialectical oppositions at whose roots lay foundational shifts in consciousness. This is the level of conversion from one foundation to another, from common sense grasp to explanatory account, from unauthenticity to a deeper grasp of the nature of intelligibility, from chaos to manifolds of cosmic order which view the universe as a dynamic process with an increasingly systematic character. There is a probability of things emerging and surviving. These schemes of order are related to an order of the soul. Each of us can verify for oneself that our knowing and doing are of a certain character and that they constitute a certain ordering process. An adequate account of intelligibility seems to require such an affirmation.

The Patristic period is a manifestation of this classical worldview. It shares its strengths and weaknesses. In a word, its principal weakness lies in the fact that it is pre-critical and a later essay will expand on that particular claim in the context of medieval scholasticism.[14] Its superlative strength, however, lies in its encounter with Biblical Revelation. There it consciously and creatively transposed biblical truths into the sets of meanings and values of classical science and metaphysics. It set itself against the "naturalism" of antiquity in its teaching on grace and, in its sacramental insight, it opposed intellectually the varieties of Hellenistic, Gnostic religiosity. It affirmed the creation (as against any tendency to debase it) by attending to the nature of the relationship between reason and faith within the order of the true. It understood the intellectual life as a dimension of spirituality and integral to the personal, ecclesial, human vocation to holiness. This achievement enhanced the intelligibility of the Christian Faith. It made it possible to speak of a Christian humanism (*humanitas* or *paideia*) alongside classical humanism. In its Greek form, *paideia* was synonymous with the idea of culture as a whole. Education embraced the entire body of Greek literature. *Paideia* thus pertains to a process involving the formation of a person in terms of a normative ideal. It introduced a kind of person who represented what was best in this encounter. Classical Christian *paideia* produced Clement of Alexandria, Augustine of Hippo, Gregory Nyssa, Basil, Gregory Nazianzen, Maximus Confessor.

By and large, its experience was very impressive indeed yet not without certain difficulties. One may advert for the moment to the Augustinian legacy of the Western Church. It has produced its share of tares and weeds, for example, in the matter of double predestination and in his platonizing, not to say Manichaean attitude toward bodiliness and sex. Yet, in their way, these shortcomings are a testimony to the foundational place Patristic thought occupies within theology. Perhaps two Patristic figures will help illustrate some of these points.

Irenaeus (fl. 170-202A.D.) championed the Catholic Faith in the task of refuting Gnosticism. His basic insight understood that analogy of being, particularly in the form of Recapitulation, is the point of distinction between Catholicism and Gnosticism. This kind of analogy, which, between the created and the uncreated, posits a similarity within a greater dissimilarity, expressed the power of the Uncreated One to create and to contain and to re-create all things. This is particularly intelligible in the human dimension. The creation, in all its aspects (perhaps especially the temporal) is the visible manifestation of the invisible, unknowable God. In created existence, in created time, in created freedom and its suffering, the movement is from image to likeness and from promise to fulfillment.

Or take Origen (185-251A.D.) for example. He is brilliantly creative with a discipline of study hitched to a wild energy. The result is the feeling of careening through the worlds of exegesis, doctrine and systematics. He authors a hexapla text of the bible to assure intelligible, clear translation in passing between Hebrew and Greek. To this concern for textual clarity, he adds the exegetical methods of literary criticism and allegory. His name stamps the legacy of Biblical interpretation bequeathed to the Church – the literal level (historical), the spiritual level (the intelligible world), the tropological level (present meaningfulness) and the anagogical level (the mystical level having to do with the relevance of the future for understanding). Origen has left commentaries on almost every book of the Bible though regrettably most have not survived. What is extant is largely to be found only in the Latin translations of Rufinus. In the *Contra Celsum* and especially in his *De Principiis*, Origen sets out a doctrinal and systematic account of the Trinity, the soul, sin and virtue. He appears to have taught a doctrine of redemption in the form of *apocatastasis* that asserts the divine will to save by denying eternal punishment. His Trinitarian views centered on the intelligibility of the divine processions by making promising, suggestive references to analogous intellectual processions within human consciousness. Origen expresses a deeply biblical and Alexandrian spirituality in the view that our inner wound of love causes us to ascend through knowledge of the Word, pursuing the question 'who has wounded me so?' He was martyred in Palestine in the Decian persecution and this fact may be moot testimony to his extraordinary unity of holiness and productivity.

The Patristic period is stretched across a framework that incessantly studied the relationship between Scripture and Doctrine, ontology and history, and, finally, exegesis as symbolic and allegorical as opposed to modern and scientific. In our time, the renewal in biblical studies took place together with a simultaneous renewal in patristic studies. But still more, both courses of study have been sublated within the much larger context of a shift in consciousness from a classicist to a historicist worldview.[15] This fact seems hugely important.

ESSAY SIX: THE WAY TO NICEA(325)

There are many travelers on the road to Nicea. For all of them, the journey is undertaken in this twilight of antiquity, in the sunset of the gods. There is a Christian emperor, Constantine (272-337A.D.). Son of Constantius Chloros, Constantine was acclaimed emperor at York on the death of his father. In 312, he defeated Maxentius at the Milvian Bridge and became emperor of the West. He owed his victory to his obeying a heavenly command given him in sleep: *In hoc signo vinces.* The sign was the *chi rho*, the two initial Greek letters of the divine name *Christos*. Accordingly, before the battle, Constantine replaced the traditional Roman cavalry standard and its pagan insignia with this *chi rho*, the Christian monogram. He believed his victory was an effect of this deed. With his accession as Emperor, Constantine legitimated the fledgling church. In fact he endowed it with privilege and acted as its patron. Eusebius (260-339) could not resist the temptation to behold in Constantine a David *Redivivus* and he elaborated a royal theology to express his vision. It celebrated one God, one Emperor, one Church. It rejoiced in a *Pax Christiana* that had supplanted the *Pax Romana*. It extolled the Christ whose reign sublated Augustus Caesar in the person and *imperium* of Constantine.[16]

Constantine ruled from the city that bears his name. Constantinople is the agreeable, new imperial city, the New Rome, indeed, the Second Rome. Lying astride the Bosporus and the Sea of Marmara (ancient Propontis), it is the link between Europe and Asia. Across the strait, lay Nicea in Bithynia, a modest distance from the capital. Its lakeside setting and imperial summer residence must have afforded a pleasant welcome to visitors. The place, if not the occasion, was a particularly enjoyable venue in which to spend a few weeks in the early summer of 325.

The mention of Bithynia and this twilight of antiquity suggest how ancient is this part of the world. For a thousand years, Greek and Hellenistic culture has been in place here, preserving the memory of Priam's Troy. Its venerable ruins in fact lay adjacent to Bithynia. This humane and energetic culture was vigorous with a full dose of self-confidence. The church is part of this world. Towards the end of his reign, Constantine may well have thought it was also too much of this world.

The issues that lay before the Council of Nicea are already rooted in a New Testament that witnesses to a Christ both human and divine. In his humanity, Christ takes human birth. He bleeds and suffers. He is crucified, dead, buried. He eats, weeps, teaches. In his divinity, Christ heals, forgives, exercises divine authority. In his person, he imparts the Spirit who is the grace of adoption. In Christ, all the fullness of God was pleased to dwell.

These affirmations raised new and further questions. If he is human, how can he be divine? If he is divine, how does he relate to Adonai, the Lord of Israel, the One God? Are they the same? If not, are there now two gods? Or is Christ perhaps a prophet, an angel, a demigod? In other words, how does one account for the New Testament data? This last question intends an explanatory grasp of the data as true. However, an explanatory account always generates its own sets of terms and relations and these terms and relations never look like the data they explain. This truth cannot be expressed too often since it accounts for the whole relationship between Scripture and Doctrine.

The initial attempts at explanatory account were awkward and sometimes clearly wrong. For example, Origen taught that the Son is God, but that the Father is "the" God. In this view, Origen has likely brought the whole subordinationist and adoptionist tradition to its climax. Sabellius had taught that the Son and the Father are really one and the same in the sense that there is no real distinction between them, no real distinction within God. The Son is just a "relational" mode of the Father. These positions did not account satisfactorily for the faith of the Church regarding Jesus Christ, a faith rooted in the data of the New Testament. For about 200 years, we have the uneasy experience of a liturgy worshipping Christ as divine (as one reads, for example, in letter X of Pliny the Younger to Trajan) and a systematic understanding unable to escape subordinationism.

On this reading, one may actually credit Arius with a keen mind temperamentally hostile toward woolly thinking. He fashioned a pointed question, 'is the Son a creature or not?' The question is shaped by a metaphysical truth, namely, that the gap between the created and the uncreated is never bridged from the creature's side and that it is therefore mythical to speak of mortals who become gods or of gods who visit us in human aspect. To his own very good question, however, Arius answered that Christ is a creature. Nothing more. Behold a greater than Solomon, a greater than Jonah. We may add a greater than Socrates, but a creature all the same and, metaphysically, nothing more than a man. One can already hear the rioting along the docks of Alexandria when this was preached from the pulpit. When Bishop Alexander of Alexandria was satisfied that Arius in fact denied the co-eternity of the Father and Son, he banished the priest from his diocese (c. 318 or 319.) But Arius was well received by Catholic bishops in Palestine and elsewhere in the Levant. What was at issue?

At issue was the breakthrough to an adequate explanatory account of the descriptive language of the New Testament regarding the humanity and divinity of Jesus Christ. Arius forced the issue because he knew, so to say, that attempts at explanatory account were to date inadequate and fuzzy in their thinking. So we must attempt to trace a line through the enormous amount of material at hand and try to make our own way intelligently to Nicea. The principals are Arius and Athanasius. Is the Son a creature or not? Immediately, appeal is made to Scripture. There are two celebrated Arian texts. The first, Prov 8, reads that the Lord created me at the beginning of his ways. In fact, the reference is to wisdom, but since Paul identified Christ as the wisdom of God, the reference must then apply to the status of Christ as created. The text clearly teaches that Wisdom Christ is created and as a creature Christ cannot then be divine. The other text comes from the Fourth Gospel in which Jesus acknowledges that "the Father is greater than I (Jn 14:28)." Taken together, Arius argued that these texts teach the subordination of the Son as a creature to the uncreated Father.

Athanasius had his stock of biblical references too, but he seemed to attach particular emphasis to the proposition that "The Father and I are One (Jn 10:30)". Clearly an identity between the two is set forth here.

What is one to do with all this apparently contradictory Scripture? Pile up some more verses? At the end of the day, clarity seemed best served by transposing the key and heading for an explanatory grasp.

The breakthrough was expressed in the term *homoousios*. It means "same being" or "same substance". It teaches an identity in divinity between the Father and the Son. The term was proposed by the emperor, surely no small mark in its favor. Nevertheless, it encountered the considerable difficulty that it was nowhere to be found in Scripture. Athanasius essentially argued its merit as making the relationship of Father and Son intelligible as both substantial and eternal and thus capable of being affirmed as true. The issue was not whether the term was in Scripture. It wasn't. At least, it was not in Scripture the way I am in this room. But it was in Scripture analogous to the way explanatory grasp (in this case, *homoousios*) is in the materials to be understood (in this case, the descriptive understanding of Scripture). To grasp the burden of that sentence is to grasp the whole Catholic understanding of the relationship between Scripture and Doctrine.

Athanasius gave his own definition of the intelligibility of *homoousios*. The term says that, whatever we affirm about the Father, the same we affirm about the Son except that the Son is Son and not Father. This teaching of the Council of Nicea was formulated in its Creed: "We believe in…Jesus Christ…begotten and not made (or created)…one in being (consubstantial or *homoousios*) with the Father."

Homoousios was offered as the answer to the question "How is Jesus both human and divine?" Jesus Christ is *homoousios* with the Father in his divinity and *homoousios* with us in his humanity. The doctrine functions logically as a principle of identity with the Father in divinity and with us in humanity. It thus affirms a metaphysically real identity in the order of existence. As true, the doctrine guides one's understanding of Scripture. Whatever else the two Arian texts referred to earlier may mean, on the terms of the *homoousios* doctrine, they cannot be understood to deny the divinity of the Son. In some ways, the doctrine is minimalistic in the extreme, a remarkably efficient term. It says little enough. But what it does say seems important. Namely, that unless the relation of Father and Son is something eternally true in God, the relation of our sonship and daughtership to God cannot be properly realized. For our relationship with the Father is completely "in the Son." This, in turn, infers a complete doctrine of the Trinity because it says something real and true about God's life, about divine sharing and relatedness and it does so by implication. Like any good answer, it soon led to a good question. Let us grant that Jesus Christ is both intelligibly human and divine inasmuch as the principle of identity is intelligible or inasmuch as one understands that immaterial generation must terminate in consubstantial being. Let us grant too that humanity and divinity are not simply the same thing. How then does one account for the unity of the divine and human in him? And that question puts many travelers on the road from Nicea to Chalcedon.[17]

ESSAY SEVEN: THE WAY TO CHALCEDON (451)

On one view, Chalcedon is not very far away from Nicea. It too is in Bithynia though it lies just across the Bosporus from Constantinople. It was a pleasant suburb of the imperial capital with its panoramic view of the Golden Horn and Santa Sophia. Today Chalcedon is a working-class inner suburb of Istanbul. On a different view, however, there is a period of 125 years between Nicea and Chalcedon. During this time, the imperial attitude toward doctrinal matters had undergone some significant shifts. For example, Constantine's own son, Constantius II, embraced Arian Christianity and brought the imperial authority to bear against Nicene Christianity. This accounts for the periods of exile and the general turbulence of Athanasius' life. Constantius appointed Arian bishops to Alexandria, Antioch and Constantinople. This period of "Arian" emperors was followed by the pagan resurgence under Julian the "Apostate" (360-363). It is only with Theodosius I that a particularly strong and vigorous Catholic emperor is returned (379-395). This epoch also frames the "Golden Age" of Patristic literature.

So many of the greats are here: the Cappadocians, Jerome, Augustine, the Cyrils, Ambrose, Hilary. This flowering implicitly testifies to the quite considerable institutional strengths of the Church throughout the Mediterranean area. These strengths contrast sharply with the shrinking and imminent collapse of the Western Roman Empire. It seems to be awaiting an inevitable fate – not "if" but "when." The great movement of Germans, Huns, Slavs and Celts is like a cresting wave. A new order is upon us. In the *City of God*, Augustine gave the Church a kind of psychological permission to go it alone without the empire and to evangelize these vast and varied peoples.

Christology with Lonergan and Balthasar

A question formed the conclusion to the previous essay. It was prompted by the teachings of the Council of Nicea. The data were that Jesus Christ is identical with the Father in divinity and identical with us in humanity. Presumably, humanity and divinity are not the same thing. How are they united in Jesus Christ?

The first attempt at an answer is located in the theological school of Alexandria, Egypt. It put forward what the tradition has called a *Logos-sarx* or a Word/flesh christology. This is a slightly different phrasing of the data of the divine and human in Christ. The tag *Logos/sarx* is mostly significant in that it was probably unsurprising that the Alexandrian tradition should eventually find its representative in the person of Apollinaris (about 315-392). It was his view that the union of the divine and human in Christ took the form of the union of the Eternal Logos with human flesh. This is awkward since flesh may be understood to be different from person. But then Apollinaris added that this union took the place of a human soul in Christ. This teaching seemed to deny the humanity of Christ by virtue of depriving him of a human soul. Can one be really human without a soul? Even if one could, would Jesus' humanity be identical with ours (with our human soul) as seems required by the *homoousios* doctrine of Nicea? And, if Jesus' humanity and ours are no longer identical, how is one to understand the doctrine of Redemption that teaches that we are saved by Christ's humanity?

A second theological school that attempted to answer the question of Christ's personal unity lay in Antioch on the Orontes in the Roman Province of Syria. It chiefly differed from Alexandria in that the Antiochenes developed a *Logos/anthropos* or a Word/human being christology. As this tag indicates, they taught the union of the Eternal Logos with a complete, full human existence. This was a felicitous and promising development. But the tensions within it are represented by its tendency to a christological dualism. This is well illustrated in the case of Nestorius (about 381-451). The great patriarch of Constantinople denied that Mary was properly called the "Mother of God." She was properly only the mother of the man Jesus. Nestorius could not establish more than a moral union between the divine and human in Jesus. The view seems to be that in Jesus the divine and human are united like oil and water. No matter how much it is shaken up, so to say, the elements eventually settle out. On one reading (perhaps too indebted to Cyril of Alexandria?), Nestorius would not accept a real union, a personal union of the two. And that of course is exactly the issue – the nature of the personal unity that is Jesus Christ. Nestorius held more to a moral union, while the Great Church sought a deeper, more ontological union. One may perhaps mention here Eutyches who applied a kind of logic to this impasse. The unity of Jesus Christ is neither according to the Alexandrian (Apollinarian) understanding nor according to the Nestorian understanding. Eutyches seemed to favor the view that Christ's unity was a *tertium quid*, a blend perhaps of the divine and human, but not properly God or man.

These various answers to the question of Christ's personal unity were conducted amid political and social turbulence of which they were often enough the cause – deposing bishops, various and often mutual condemnations, the convoking of regional synods, questions of authority and the imperial duty to keep the peace. Finally, a Council was convoked at Chalcedon. It situated itself in the line of Nicea, repeating and affirming the full *homoousios* doctrine. Here is the relevant section of the Chalcedonian definition:

> "One and the same Christ, Son, Lord, Only begotten, made known in two natures which exist without confusion, without change, without division, without separation; the difference of the natures having been in no way taken away by reason of their union, but rather the properties of each being preserved, and both concurring into one Person (prosopon) and one hypostasis – not parted or divided into two persons (prosopa), but one and the same Son and Only-begotten, the divine Logos, the Lord Jesus Christ."[18]

This is the Chalcedonian, orthodox answer to the question 'what is the personal unity of Jesus Christ?' Its answer is often referred to in shorthand as the 'one Person in two natures' doctrine.

This definition is very much in the realm of explanatory grasp. What does Chalcedon mean by "Person"? For Chalcedon and its intellectual world, "person" is unintelligible apart from a "nature." Nature is the source of activity, the principle of operating, of thinking and of consciousness and a nature is rooted in "person" as the underlying principle of individuality and oneness. Person here does not act nor is it conscious. Such a view is quite opposed to a modern definition of person as a self-conscious center of activity. Person makes human nature to be concrete, to be this particular person. Regarding the unity of Christ, the definition posits one person who is the Incarnate second person (or *hypostasis*) of the Divine Trinity and in this person there exist two natures. There is a human nature that is more or less the locus for our modern understanding of a human being or person and there is a divine nature. There are two natures because the human and the divine are not the same thing. "Person" answers to the question 'what is there one of in Jesus Christ?' and "natures" answer to the question 'what are there two of in Jesus Christ?'

What does one understand about Jesus Christ on the basis of this classic Chalcedonian definition of one divine Person with a human nature and a divine nature? The definition affirms that Christ is fully God (against Arius) and fully man (against Appolinaris), indivisibly one (against Nestorius) yet without confusion (against Eutyches). Chalcedon affirms that human existence is constituted by its relationship with God. It is a relationship characterized by the polarity of unity and diversity between the created and the uncreated and this polarity may be further differentiated in terms of the sets male and female, heaven and earth, nature and grace. By our growth in love, this relationship may be seen to divinize our humanity.

Once again, one may note that the Chalcedonian definition is spare and minimal, that it employs Greek metaphysical terms and relations, but that it applies them to serving the intelligibility of Divine, Biblical Revelation concerning Jesus Christ. As such this is a foundational example of Catholic systematic theology that stands to doctrine as understanding stands to truth. For all that, one cannot overlook the fact that the definition was not universally received in the East although it clearly was in the West. Egypt never accepted it and Nestorian Christianity spread eastward to the roof of Asia. So far from assuring religious and therefore political unity in the empire, it seemed to aggravate its basic tensions and strains. In fact, their resolution came, not from doctrinal unity, but from the appearance of Islam whose conquest of the whole area made moot many points of doctrinal unity and imperial policy.

This essay has tried to steer a path through the dense modern scholarship on the question of Chalcedon and on the evidence it suggests for a new view of Nestorius, Eutyches and Cyril of Alexandria. Much Patristic research is concentrated here and indeed on the whole question of Arius and in time its results may qualify the perspectives represented here in important ways. So far, however, that research seems to confirm the basic direction undertaken here in retrieving the questions and tracing the basic growth in explanatory grasp with its sets of terms and relations drawn from attending to data and correctly understanding it. Modern research uncovers a number of historical difficulties. One challenge for the Ancient Church lay in getting right acceptable terms and relations to express Christological doctrine. Another challenge had to do with minting accurate Latin equivalents of Greek technical terms. At the end of the day, Chalcedon defined "how" Jesus Christ is one yet really human and really divine. In that lies its strength. But for some the famous definition has produced a Hellenized, nonbiblical Christ. That issue forms the substance of the next essay.

ESSAY EIGHT: OBJECTIONS AND DIFFICULTIES WITH "CHALCEDONIAN" CHRISTOLOGY

Nearly fifty years ago, a Dutch Jesuit, Father Piet Schoonenberg, brought out a book entitled *The Christ*. In it he set forth a series of criticisms of Chalcedon. Its doctrine, he wrote, was too abstract. It ignored the radical dissimilarity between the divine and human natures so that they were viewed as somehow "competing" with each other. As a result, the definition ironically came to be understood in a Monophysite sense in the tradition of Apollinaris, though here the issue was the confusion between the one divine Person and the one divine Nature of Chalcedon. The ontology of its definition of the constitution of Christ as one Person in two Natures had no need or desire to refer to the particular, historical Jesus of the gospels. Chalcedon's doctrinal Christ did not need a biblical Christ. It was Schoonenberg's view that the Chalcedonian definition has essentially hobbled the tradition right down the line and that the task now, though he did not use the word, was to deconstruct Chalcedon by advancing a new starting point for Christology: begin with the human being Jesus of Nazareth; reflect on the completeness of his humanity; and consider that his humanity must have everything that essentially constitutes the human. That will be the context for considering Jesus' divinity or pre-existence. With his book, Schoonenberg opened a fresh dialogue on Christology.

Schoonenberg's criticisms are important and invite larger comment. These essays have already touched on some aspects. The first essay, on sources and methods, indicated the significance of modern, scientific, historical-critical methods while the essay on Patristic christology identified the distinction between classicism and historicity. These perspectives are relevant here as well. In fact, the present essay returns to the question of the significance of the shift from the classicist to historicist foundations by inquiring now into the relevance of modernity and particularly the way in which it has helped shape modern Christology.

Karl Jaspers believed that history is marked by shifts in intellectual consciousness that he named axial periods. The Greek intellectual breakthrough is a splendid example of such a shift and its development is characterized by the achievement of a more and more conscious grasp of the distinction between philosophy, history and science on the one hand and myth and magic on the other. Or, put differently, the Greek breakthrough stands on a conscious grasp, within intellectual consciousness, of the distinction between understanding as descriptive and understanding as explanatory. It is instructive to observe in this axial period that while Greece stands on this side of it and ancient Egypt on the other side, nevertheless Egypt appears more advanced than Greece, for example, in large-scale engineering and administration. Persia as well as the Aztec and Inca cultures of this hemisphere would be ranged with Egypt on the far side of the axial breakthrough. They are breathtaking cultures as we know and there is no desire to be ungracious in situating them on the other side of that axial period. But the story of classical Greece is, in Bruno Snell's felicitous phrase,[19] the discovery of mind. This way of putting the matter is relevant to Father Schoonenberg's critique of Chalcedon.

The shift to modernity passes through medieval scholasticism. Its considerable achievement is to have developed a full metaphysical context for the methodical and systematic expression of faith. Its recurring acts of understanding as conscious and explanatory were expressed in the sets of terms and relations Scholasticism generated. It distinguished verbal, notional and real distinctions and among these it drew yet further distinctions. The breakthrough here is in terms of full systematic meaning and on this point scholasticism, perhaps especially in the form of the *quaestio disputata*, already anticipates modern scientific method, for example, in the applied fields of medieval science *(physica)* and medicine. Scholasticism took a great delight in the architecture of the mind that raised questions, defined terms, clarified relations and arrived at solutions. For all that, however, scholasticism stands on the one side of another axial breakthrough which received memorable expression, for example, in the *Organum Novum* of Francis Bacon.

Bacon appealed for an end to a kind of logic that dealt with general concepts and whose tool was the syllogism. He argued in favor of gathering data, devising experiments, formulating hypotheses and verifying results. He represents the ongoing discovery of mind. If the view he represents is widened it will, I think, be seen that one cannot bring over to modernity certain features that were dear to those on the far side of the breakthrough he represents. So, for example, the Greek and medieval notions of metaphysics or science cannot be brought over to modernity. Aristotle framed his fundamental understanding and its originality and synthesizing power is still impressive. But it is on the far side of the breakthrough into modernity.

For Aristotle viewed science as certain knowledge through their causes of what is universal and necessary. These causes were named end, agent, matter and form. But modern science, in all its fields, deals not with the certain but the probable, not so much with causes as with correlations. It tends to data, not to things and, because its results are not necessary, modern science verifies them. Scientific facts are verified explanations. Modern theoretically differentiated consciousness did not happen all at once. Thus, it was only non-Euclidean geometry that allowed mathematicians to acknowledge that their postulates or axioms were not necessary truths. It was quantum theory that allowed physicists to set aside talk about the necessary laws of nature. It was the Great Depression of the thirties that allowed economists to abandon the notion of the iron laws of economics.

Again, Aristotle acknowledged special sciences and a general science, metaphysics, that dealt with being as being, but he went on to define metaphysics as the general case of the content of the other sciences. As a result, all the sciences drew their own sets of terms and relations from metaphysics. On this side of the breakthrough, metaphysics is understood not as the general case of the content of the other sciences, but as the general case of the methods of the sciences. And this breakthrough is conscious.

Modern consciousness distinguishes logical and metaphysical contexts from the historical context that provides evidence for critical understanding and its historical-critical methods. It goes on to distinguish differentiated from undifferentiated consciousness, a world of immediacy from a world mediated by meaning and metaphysics from scientific method. This capacity to make these conscious distinctions allows one to relate intelligently one historical context with another, and this allows one to encounter a truth or a number of truths that extend over places and times.

The title of the present essay indicates a commitment to speak about obstacles and difficulties associated with the Chalcedonian definition. For Father Schoonenberg and others, the definition of One Divine Person with a divine nature and a human nature suffers from a particularly virulent piece of Hellenization and an unbiblical mentality. While this may in fact be true, it need not be. Consider the progress of the questions asked at that time, namely, is Jesus truly human and divine? Yes, says the *homoousios* doctrine. If humanity and divinity are not the same thing (and clearly they are not) what unites them? Chalcedon answers that the two natures concur in a single Divine Person. Clearly this definition presumed familiarity with the intellectual consciousness of antiquity. Without it, one may well embrace, unbeknownst, a monophysitism that, among other things, ravages a doctrine of Redemption and blocks one's reading the gospels for their portrait of Jesus. But if one rehearses the questions for oneself and if one learns the sets of terms and relations in its metaphysical context, it is possible to be orthodox in faith and biblical in inspiration. It is possible to understand Chalcedon to mean that Jesus' human nature is constituted in its being gathered up into the service of the Father. Here humanity is not affirmed by appealing to some sort of autonomy that denies the divine. Nor is humanity denied by affirming the divine as though, like Icarus, human existence would melt in destruction as it approached God. In this sense, the Icarus myth is of a piece with monophysitism and monothelitism. Chalcedon affirms that to be created and human requires relatedness to God. In this affirmation lies the whole gospel life of free obedience and self-denial in order to be a disciple of Jesus.

Arguably, this is the intelligibility of Chalcedon. But is such a retrieval too fussy and unworkable? Father Schoonenberg thought it was and he wrote a thoughtful book to that effect. The task of retrieval, however, will be rewarded if Chalcedon becomes for the inquirer not only true but meaningful.

Where considerable difficulty does exist, however, is in the deficiency of the psychology available to Chalcedon. Its terms and relations are taken from Aristotelian metaphysics with its a priori perfections of potency, form and act as the essential attributes of the soul. These premises have led the tradition to maintain logically that Jesus possessed the perfection of human knowledge at every moment. As a result, on Christmas morning, the babe knew the laws of thermodynamics as well as the plot of your favorite novel. Clearly such a viewpoint sits awkwardly to the truth of Christ's humanity. The way forward has perhaps already been indicated. One must try and see the deficiency in a metaphysical psychology and, with modern psychology, recognize a new set of terms and relations. For example, modern psychology understands and explains the definition of a person as the subject of interpersonal relations, human development as occurring in a symbolic world mediated by meaning, and the significance of the distinction between speaking of a human being and speaking of a human person. In particular, the next essay looks set to illustrate these points particularly in its discussion of consciousness and knowledge in Jesus Christ. One hopes such terms and relations will illumine the intelligibility of Jesus Christ in a particularly modern way. It will be consistent with the critical evidence of the New Testament itself which teaches that he is like us in all things but sin and that he grew in wisdom, age and grace before all.[20]

PART III

ESSAY NINE: THE KNOWLEDGE AND SELF-CONSCIOUSNESS OF JESUS AND SOME RELATED POINTS

Jesus Christ is truly divine and truly human. Setting the first point to one side for the moment, the affirmation of his humanity allows us to affirm in him the fact of a normal cognitional development. And on this score there is ample Biblical data: "But about that day or hour no one knows, neither the angels in heaven, **nor the Son**, but only the Father (Mk 13:32)." Or again: "When Jesus heard him {the Centurion}, **he was amazed**, and said to those who followed him, 'Truly I tell you, in no one in Israel have I found such faith' (Mt 8: 10)." Here Jesus' surprise appears to indicate that he did not know of the faith of the pagan Centurion beforehand. Similarly, we read: "And **he was amazed** at their unbelief (Mk 6:6)." Here Jesus is clearly taken unawares by their unbelief. A final, well-known example may suffice: "And Jesus increased in wisdom and in years, and in divine and human favor (Lk 2:52)." These factors witness to a normal, human cognitional development. The burden of what follows will be to draw on the resources of Bernard Lonergan and Hans Urs Von Balthasar to cast light on the issues treated in the present essay. Let us begin with Lonergan.

What is the effect on these remarks when one says that Jesus Christ, One and the Same, is also truly divine? Does he know with the knowledge of God? "Now we know that you know all things, and do not need to have anyone question you; by this we believe that you came from God (Jn 16:30)." Put differently, how can Jesus know something in his divine nature and not know the same thing in his human nature?

These questions intend the systematic exigence of the question, 'what does it mean for a divine person to live a fully human life (that is, 'to come into the world', cf Jn 1:9; Heb 10:5)?'

Underlying these questions is the realm of consciousness. Consciousness is the self-experience of a subject as subject in its acts and states and while these acts and states vary over time the subject remains consciously the same. Still, one may object that it is one thing to be conscious of oneself as God and something quite different to be conscious of oneself as a man. So can divine consciousness and human consciousness reveal one and the same subject? Yes. And this point can be illustrated by adding an analogy to the definition of consciousness. It is one thing to enjoy a good dinner and quite another thing to be executed but one and the same subject can enjoy the one and undergo the other. This is the case because consciousness reveals not only acts and states but also the subject and, while acts and states vary, the subject remains consciously the same.

Consciousness reveals the subject as constituted in its acts and as **coming to know** the subject (or the self) that consciousness reveals. On this view there is a distinction between consciousness and knowledge since knowledge is a compound of attending, understanding and judging. Christ is eternally the subject of divine consciousness — of Trinitarian Love, of Himself as the Father's Word and as Sent by the Father to the world. In the gospels this constitutes his sense of mission. This divine consciousness judges Trinitarian filiation as valuable and as true. It judges Love proceeding from the Father and the Son as valuable and true as the Holy Spirit. The supposition here is that the human distinction between consciousness and knowledge points analogously to some such similar distinction within God. The theological tradition of the psychological analogy and the doctrinal tradition of Chalcedon confirm the reasonableness of affirming in God some such distinction between consciousness and knowledge. In other words, the divine consciousness is the self-experience of the subject as subject, an experience inherent in each of the subject's acts or actions. In time and in history, the divine consciousness of the Eternal Son became the subject of a human consciousness in Jesus Christ.

As the Incarnate Logos, Jesus Christ also possesses a human preconceptual and undifferentiated consciousness of himself as the divine Person of the Word. Equally, as the Incarnate Logos, he possesses knowledge of the divine essence through the beatific vision.

For the beatific vision grasps properly and without analogy the full intelligibility of *quid sit Deus* (the divine essence). This constitutes the primary object of the beatific vision. The secondary objects of the beatific vision are "realities of the created order in so far as they lie within the divine power and the divine will. One cannot know that power and that will in the divine essence without in some way knowing these secondary objects."[21] So it is also true to say that the vision of God is also a matter of Christ's finite human knowledge as distinct from his divine knowledge. The claim then is that Jesus Christ knows who God is and what the divine essence is. The Gospel is open to the view that at some point in his ministry, relating his human self-consciousness and the beatific vision, Jesus concluded that the Son of God whom he knows through the beatific vision and his own self of whom he is aware in his human consciousness are one and identical. Such a self-affirmation may underlie the accounts of his baptism or perhaps in his response to Peter's confession of faith. Put differently, there is a distinction between the beatific vision of the Logos incarnate in Jesus and Jesus' human consciousness. This distinction pertains to a subjectivity expressed on the one hand through human acts of understanding and on the other to the fact of the hypostatic union which is subsequently grasped as his personal unity by his conscious affirming that what he has come to understand over time is in fact true.

In the main, the foregoing represents the direction Bernard Lonergan has laid out.[22] By contrast, he seemed to hold the view that Rahner understates the distinction and overdraws the relationship between consciousness and reflexive knowledge in God. Rahner did not quite work out a general account of consciousness and knowledge and this can be seen in a slightly eager tendency to pull consciousness into a type of knowing.[23]

Let us take stock. Lonergan has made the case that in Jesus Christ there is (1) a divine consciousness, (2) a divine knowledge of the divine essence (the beatific vision) and, (3) that, historically, this divine consciousness and divine knowledge became one and identical with the subject of a human intellectual consciousness and that this unity or identity is named Jesus Christ. A relevant and rough proportion seems to be that in him the divine stands to the human as consciousness stands to knowledge. And human consciousness stands to knowledge as conscious acts of attending, understanding and judging stand to what is true and therefore known in normal human cognitional development.

But this is only a proportion. It should in no way obscure the truth that no-one knows the Father except the Son. And the singular nature of such knowing presumably stems from the beatific vision. Yet, as the unity of the human and the divine, while Jesus knows the Father, this knowledge is properly knowledge under the conditions of normal human cognitive development. This must be the case lest another truth be denied, namely, that no one knows the Father except the Son and **anyone to whom the Son wishes to reveal him.** For, presumably, the knowledge of the Father that the Son reveals to us is not simply identical with the knowledge proper to the beatific vision.

What did Jesus know and when did he know it? Lonergan concludes that Jesus knew the beatific vision in the manger in a way proper to his divine consciousness. The divine essence is the primary object of the beatific vision. But Jesus came to **know** who he was as God in terms of a normal human cognitive development. For this reason he never came to know the laws of thermodynamics or the plot of that novel you read last summer at the beach. For neither the knowledge proper to the beatific vision nor normal human cognitional development, tied as it is to specific historical and cultural contexts, allows for it. Yet he is God from God and Light from Light. And it must be said that these several conclusions are completely in keeping with the full and integral truth of Chalcedonian and Catholic Faith. This is a point Fr. Lonergan makes eloquently:

> "The main parallel statements are that, as there is one person with a divine and a human nature, so there is one subject with a divine and a human consciousness. As the person, so also the subject is without division or separation. As the two natures, so also the divine and human consciousness is without confusion or interchange. As the person so also the subject is a divine reality. As the human nature, so also the human consciousness is assumed. As there is a great difference between 'being god' and 'being a man,' so also there is a great difference between 'being conscious of oneself as God' and 'being conscious of oneself as man.' As the former difference is surmounted hypostatically by union in the person, so the latter difference is surmounted hypostatically by union in the subject. As the two natures do not

prove two persons, so the divine and the human consciousness do not prove two subjects."[24]

A quite different account of the knowledge and self-consciousness of Jesus has been presented by Hans Urs Von Balthasar as part of his project of constructing a Theo-Drama. Philosophy and Theology give properly different accounts of knowing. Philosophy, however, does not know the divine essence whereas Theology knows the Trinitarian love as visible and crucified. And the key term here is 'mission.'

With Jesus, 'mission' embraces the universal eschatological task that is undertaken within a limited human existence. Thus, mission is the key to the movement from what Jesus does to who Jesus is and that movement will appreciate that in Jesus we encounter "someone who never was, and never could have been, anyone other than the One Sent."[25] In other words, can Jesus be sent in such an absolute sense that his mission (his being sent) so coincided with his person that both together constitute God's exhaustive self-communication? Here attention shifts from the question of what he knew to the conditions that made it possible for what empirically took place in him.

Jesus' mission (he is the '*apostolos'*, Heb 3:1) is indicated in the terms 'son' or 'beloved son' or God's 'own' son (Rom 8:3). Such terms serve to distinguish Jesus from the prophetic missions of old even as they prepared for his mission. They also unfold New Testament teaching along two lines. First, one's attitude toward the One Sent expresses at the same time one's attitude toward the One who sent him. Second, the One Sent comes to serve us, to seek, save and fulfill.

Jesus' mission is clearly expressed at his baptism as Son and in a number of baptismal texts where person and mission are identified. For example, "I have a baptism with which to be baptized, and what stress I am under until it is completed (Lk 12:50)!" Or again, "For the Son of Man came not to be served but to serve, and to give his life as a ransom for many (Mk 10:45)." Here there is laid out a proper and strict identity between the person and mission of Jesus, the beloved Son. The Son is entirely identified with his work in the world. The New Testament therefore indicates that Jesus' relationship to his mission goes beyond all biblical precedent even as its full dimensions only unfold in him over time.

Here we may speak of a divine element which is unique and which is disclosed in Jesus' consciousness as the One Sent. Balthasar has named this Jesus' "mission-consciousness." The divine element disclosed in that mission-consciousness is also defined and limited by that mission-consciousness. This mission-consciousness is not imposed on Jesus from outside since his self-consciousness is identical with his mission. Neither is there a time when Jesus did not possess this mission-consciousness. He is this mission already in his eternal procession from the Father. This mission-consciousness embraces at the same time both the presence of the One Who Sends (the Father) and the temporal and developmental quality of a mission received and implemented by a human being ("Jesus increased in wisdom and in years and in divine and human favor," Lk 2:52). Jesus' person and mission are identical in origin in the Father and their identity continues in the temptations Jesus experiences, in his life of prayer and in a life of faith that is proper to him as Son, namely, that he has been sent by the Father. Such an identity expresses the fact that the Father is completely manifested in the mission of the Son and that this fact in turn completely characterizes the self-consciousness of the Son. "Who do you say I am?" You are the one sent by the Father, the Word, the Son, who makes the Father known. Put differently, the human consciousness and the divine consciousness coincide in Jesus in terms of mission, in terms of himself as the one sent by the Father. This is also something true, something Jesus knows and affirms.

The conscious subject knows that he is such. He knows he is human in a unique and incomparable way. But does he also know who he is? That is, does he know that he is not only quantitatively but also qualitatively different from all other conscious subjects? How does the conscious subject know the self to be a person? Balthasar earnestly makes the point that a conscious subject is properly called a person when God addresses that conscious subject, revealing who the subject is, what meaning the subject has for the God of truth. God shows the conscious subject the purpose (and therefore the mission) of his conscious, human existence. We have seen that this takes place, for example, in the baptismal texts of the Gospels ("You are my beloved Son") where Jesus received his mission as Son and, as Son, his personal uniqueness that he knows to be his existence as Son. In this way, Jesus exhibits the movement from being a conscious subject to being a person in the knowledge of who he is. And, while only in Jesus do we find an identity between his consciousness and his mission, still there exists an analogy whereby we can know that in him we pass from being conscious subjects to being persons. The more we are "in Him", the deeper will be our definition of being a person and the greater will be our understanding of our mission, our being sent in this world. In other words, every conscious subject is created for the sake of a mission and it is that mission that makes him or her a person. We can see this, for example, in the case of Paul. Jesus has claimed Paul's existence as a conscious subject, but he has expropriated Paul in order to personalize him by assigning him a mission.

Jesus experiences his human consciousness entirely in terms of mission with the attendant ideas of obedience and salvation. For this reason, there is not a twofold consciousness in the Incarnate Logos and it is on this point that our two authors seem most to diverge from each other. The mission of which Jesus is aware is the mission of the Only Son. He knows that, as man, he freely does what, as Logos, he wills to do. Put differently, the man Jesus knows that what he freely does is done by the Son of God.

What else comes into view when one situates Jesus' knowledge and consciousness in the passage from subject to person who knows the self as one sent in Christ? First, the movement toward becoming a person points to the dignity of human nature as given in an individual, human, personal existence. This truth allows the second dimension of his mission-consciousness, the *admirabile commercium*, to come into view, the wondrous exchange of our death for his life. For it is not a human nature that lives or dies but a human being. A third dimension is expressed by St. Paul as being *in Christo* and that is the effect of grace taking hold of one as a conscious subject, expropriating one and making one a person by being sent into the world (mission). Thus, one becomes a brother or sister of the 'first-born' (Rom 8:29). The final dimension of his mission-consciousness touches upon the cosmic attributes of Jesus' primacy, his predestined role, his pre-existence and his role as mediator. As the Last Adam, he recapitulates all things in himself. He is the Lamb slain from the foundation of the world who yet ushers in the end of the ages.

Lonergan has expressed his understanding of consciousness with the term conscientia-experientia[26] (consciousness as experience) by which he holds that everything known is known insofar as it is in act – not insofar as it is an object. In this view, the subject is known together with knowledge of objects. Conscientia-experientia meets Balthasar's mission-consciousness (the identity of Jesus' mission and consciousness) and these are the two relevant terms that have emerged in this essay. With them we enter upon the mind of Christ (Phil 2:5). In part, the content of these terms is common and shared, namely, that Christ's consciousness embraces Trinitarian love and Himself as both the Father's Word and as the One Sent (his Mission) by the Father to the world to redeem it. In part, these terms embrace different contents. Lonergan remains within the cognitional framework he has classically elaborated to ground and explain the relationship of consciousness and knowledge in Jesus Christ. Balthasar has grounded personhood and consciousness in the data of Scripture. At the end of the day, however, they have both responded to the same question, namely, what does it mean for a divine person to live a truly human life?

ESSAY TEN: FEMINISM AND CHRISTOLOGY

Christian feminism represents a liberation from the sexism that, in its view, has grievously distorted the whole Christian tradition. This distortion ranges across historical, theological and biblical dimensions. It even extends to Christology so that feminism seeks liberation from the story of the male liberator. Christian feminism seeks to liberate chiefly women, but everyone in fact, from the sexist patriarchalism that prevents women and men from achieving their proper liberation in terms of correct consciousness and equality. By contrast, it wishes to offer the tools to critique properly sources and hermeneutical issues in order to contribute toward this liberation.

Such a view establishes a common ground for what are otherwise different perspectives within Christian feminism. For example, in her book *Beyond God the Father,*[27] Mary Daly held that the male symbols of God and Savior as well as the ultimate symbol of the "all-male" Trinity with its procession of a divine son from a divine father are radically inadequate symbols for women. This seems, on balance, to represent an extreme view though one should not on that account isolate the work or the author from what is a crowded field of contributors. In fact, many Christian feminists believe they recognize the blighted fruit of a diseased tree when they see it and many of them agree that the biblical male symbols have in fact legitimated the historical subordination of women.

There is, in fact, a daunting amount of scholarship associated with Feminism, Christology and related theological fields. This fact is on a par with feminist research across the humanities and extending even into the sciences where, for example, the term "ecofeminism" wishes to illustrate the consequences of sexism and patriarchy in the environmental crisis. The remainder of the essay is made up of a few brushstrokes. In this connection, while I omit their foundational works, I do not wish to omit mentioning here Elizabeth Johnson and Rosemary Reuther in the matter of Feminism and Christology.

Elisabeth Schüssler Fiorenza[28] has argued that Jesus understood his "Father" primarily as gracious goodness personified in sophia/wisdom. This tradition, which also incorporates spirit/shekinah (goddess) language, provides a rich wisdom tradition of metaphors of divine **maternity** as may be seen, for example, in the manner of imparting or instilling wisdom or in the image of God as "She-who-dwells-within." Trinitarian 'generativity', with its 'begetting' by sophia-wisdom, is thus genuinely maternal. This tradition personifies divine wisdom as feminine. She was present with God at the creation, is sovereign over the whole world of nature and imparts true moral teaching.

In this view, Jesus brought 'goddess' language into the person and tradition of the God of Israel and allowed God now to be imaged in female realities. Jesus saw himself as the messenger of Sophia while others saw her in his mission and teaching. Women counted among Jesus' first missions to the Gentiles (for example, the Syrophoenician woman of Mk 7:24-30 or the Samaritan woman of Jn 4:1-42). They are to be seen at calvary ("Many women were also there," Mt 27:55). They were decisive in the witness to Easter faith ("Mary Magdalene and the other Mary were there, sitting opposite the tomb." Mt 27:61). Fiorenza takes the view that the Jesus movement freed believers from patriarchal family structure. All are now brothers and sisters, calling no one on earth their father ("Who are my mother and brothers?", Mk 3:31-35; or again, among the hundredfold in this life are "brothers and sisters and mothers", Mk 10:30). These brothers and sisters care for the children who are the little ones and who look to us, for of such as these is the kingdom of heaven. At the end of the day, this view of community understood the equality of women in their role as disciples of Jesus. The evangelizing of the gentiles was conducted under the leadership of the spirit/Sophia who makes believers to be daughters and sons and among whom, by virtue of their baptism, there is no longer slave and free, Jew and Greek, male and female – "for you are all one in Christ Jesus (Gal 3:28)." Indeed some scholars observe that leadership in St. Paul's first communities was more along the lines of preaching and teaching rather than the somewhat later priestly office of presider. And women may well have preached and taught together with

Paul: "Greet Prisca and Aquila, who work with me in Christ Jesus, who risked their necks for my life, to whom not only I give thanks but also all the churches of the Gentiles. Greet also the church in their house (Rom 16:3-5)." In any case, Fiorenza maintains, the repatriarchalizing of relationships can regrettably be seen in Ephesians, Colossians and in the pastoral letters.

A particularly fruitful line of inquiry is represented in the research of Phyllis Trible.[29] She draws attention to the basic metaphor of 'male and female together' as the image of God in the world: "So God created humankind in his image, in the image of God he created them; male and female he created them (Gen 1:27)." It is the foundational metaphor, balancing what are, by contrast, incomplete metaphors. Thus, it corrects such metaphors of God as father, mother, husband, pregnant, king, midwife. As embracing male and female, the precise connection of this foundational metaphor with the controversy over the worship of the "Queen of Heaven" (Jer 44:15-30) remains I think unclear. Some have thought the reference may point to the early worship of the Lord God of Israel together with his consort Wisdom. Perhaps his consort is better named Asherah, the ancient goddess who was mother of the gods and wife of El and who may have figured in the very ancient Yahwist cult up to the time of the Judges, about 1200-1000B.C. On this view, Jeremiah, a pre-exilic prophet, represents the patriarchal purging of the feminine, divine element of wisdom that had earlier been integral to the cult of Yahweh. Jeremiah was successful in this undertaking and the goddess dimension was integrated into the 'acceptable' image of wisdom as created and subordinate to the Creator who is presented as male. Considerable scholarly attention has been focused here and its results will doubtless prove valuable.

Trible sees the foundational metaphor of Gen 1:27 expressed in the unity of male and female who are together – in creation, in disobedience, in erotic love and joy. Some would add here that Gen 1: 26-27 is evidence for the view that the unity of male and female reflects the ancient understanding of the divine as a couple, as the Lord God together with his consort (Asherah?), who are speaking at Gen 1:26: "Let us make humankind in our image, according to our likeness…." Even the lovers in the *Song of Songs* (especially chapters 4 and 7) are thought to point to this divine couple. In any case, these are examples of "countervoices" in an otherwise patriarchal world of culture and text.

The Word of God appears in the world as a man, the "Last" Adam. Elsewhere in Scripture, the principle that comes forth from God and embodies God in creation is predominantly feminine, for example, **shekinah** (indwelling), **ruach** (spirit) and **memra** (word). But here as the "last" Adam, the Word of God is male. It is his mission to represent the Origin, his Father, in the world. Again, as the Last Adam, is he not incomplete until God forms woman taken from his side? This already points to the relevance of the Church that comes forth from his side, the Church "which is his body, the fullness of him who fills all in all (Eph 1:23)."

In the garden, Eve is taken from Adam's side and formed into woman. She is not produced by his sexual power nor, like him, taken from the dust of the earth. Thus does the sacred text teach the substantial equality and unity of man and woman. Greek theology recognizes in this the pattern of the eternal generation of the Son by the Father. The substantial equality we associate with the Trinitarian persons applies therefore to male and female in the account of the origin of Eve from the side of Adam. Neither origin from Adam's sexuality (which only expresses itself, together with death, after the Fall) nor from the dust of the earth could express this truth. For, as the product of Adam's sexuality, Eve would be inferior to him as his daughter and, as fashioned from the dust of the earth, she would possess only an external unity with him. She is the creator's gift in order to complete the man: "Male and female he created them, (Gen 1:27);" "and they become one flesh, (Gen 2:24)."

Historically and theologically, it has been heavy going to preserve this tradition from foundering in the view that the male represents spirit or heaven while the woman represents nature or earth (mater=mother =matter).[30] So for example, the superiority of the male may be seen in certain of the speeches in Plato's *Symposium*. Its setting was the feast in honor of the death of Dionysos. It lasted several days and much wine was quaffed in the god's honor. A day in the festival was set aside for speeches delivered in praise of love. Phaedrus's speech (178A-180B) begins by recalling that love (Eros) is the oldest of the gods. His greatest blessing is the love of an older man for a youth, a love that knows no shame and desires only what is noble. The bond such love establishes is best both for the city and for the army. In this form, love endures death itself. This truth, Phaedrus continues, is ably represented in Admetus and his wife Alcestis, in Orpheus and his wife Eurydice and, especially, in Achilles and Patroclus. Pausanias responds and in his speech (180C-185C) he contrasts two loves – the heavenly and the common (or popular). Common love is vulgar, bodily and possessive, for women as well as for youths. By contrast, heavenly love is without lust and is drawn to the male as superior, awaiting the male's intellectual maturity and making for thoughtfulness, friendship and camaraderie. This love is noble because it acts nobly on behalf of the noble virtue of the beloved. Such a love is honorable and esteemed by the polis. In his speech, Aristophanes (189C-193D) recounts the ancient myth of the three kinds of human beings – male, female and androgynous. Zeus was threatened by them and decided to cut them in two. For that reason each half looks for its other half. The best halves are males. We should imagine Aristophanes giving off this speech just after a bout of hiccups and sneezing that indicate that his speech is a satire or parody on the Greek tradition of the superiority of the male. These three speeches represent quite ancient, widespread and influential interpretations of the relationship between male and female. But they are not part of that biblical teaching which unites Genesis and the Letter to the Ephesians by passing straight through the form of Mary the "woman" (Jn 2: 4), "that he might present the church to himself in splendor, without spot or wrinkle or any such thing, that she might be holy and without blemish (Eph 5:27)." In other words, Mary as the mother of Christ is at the same time and by that fact the real symbol of the church as the bride of Christ. Virginity/celibacy is the New Testament grace uniting mother and bride in the fruitfulness of faith. The form of ecclesial life for both male and female is thus feminine/marian and sacramental.

This is the basis for the fact that male and female believers are equally baptized, married and take religious vows. It may also serve as the basis for a restoration of the order of deacon to women. Some may hold such a view suspect as a diversion from the real issue of the priestly ordination of women, but on its face this restoration may enjoy a liturgical and pastoral basis in Catholic antiquity. In recent years, the Holy See has expressed genuine interest in the question. There is evidence in the East that bishops ordained women to the order of deacon, that they wore the stole of that office and that this order was deeply honored. Her ministry of deacon drew her to the sanctuary for the service of the Divine Liturgy. If no obstacles lie in the way, there is an arguable advantage to opening this order to women in that it may generate new interest for admitting women to other forms of ministry, for example, lectors, teachers, administrators, healers.

The sacramental distinction of male and female, which is readily associated with marriage, is also the basis for the discipline that the office of priest is restricted to males whose gender, in grace, manifests, in the eucharist, the role of Christ as husband to the Church as bride – "This is a great mystery, and I am applying it [the spousal relationship of husband and wife] to Christ and the church (Eph 5:32)."

Some will take the view that this sacramental tradition of the sublime unity and equality of male and female has succumbed to the sin of clericalism and authoritarianism. Many more will perhaps take the view that there is underway at present a providential chastening of the priestly ministry and a conversion away from traditional temptations to power in favor of a renewed spirituality of the priesthood of the Good Shepherd who came to serve us.

A final note. Suspended above the altar in the cathedral church of St. John the Divine in New York City there is a crucified woman called "Christa." "Christa" asks the question, 'can a male Savior save women?' Would it, for example, make any difference if Jesus had been a woman? These questions seem to have generated two types of answer. The first distinguished Jesus' sex from his humanity as represented in the ancient view of Redemption, namely, that what was not assumed was not redeemed. This doctrine avoids both a docetic and a sexist (male) Christ while holding to the doctrine of Christ as Savior. And, on this view, a human Christ (as distinct from a male Christ) annuls the sacramental requirement that there can only be a male priesthood. The second answer views Jesus as androgynous (for example, Jesus as mother) and this view helps integrate the feminine into Jesus. These two types of answer are not without their difficulties. Really, what sort of distinction is represented by a human Christ as opposed to a male Christ? But, presumably, these answers allow many women and men to understand that Jesus Christ is authentically their Savior and to embrace that truth.

ESSAY ELEVEN: CHRISTOLOGY AND THE LIBERATION OF PEOPLES

An ancient principle of ecclesiology may serve as an introduction to the basic ideas of liberation theology. The principle reads: *ecclesia semper reformanda.* It enshrines the quest for a church that is truly catholic, evangelical and reformed ("hear what the Spirit is saying to the churches," Rev 2:7). As a principle, it has been widely applied within liberation theology. For example, Leonardo Boff has sharply contrasted the view that the church is the community of Christ through the Holy Spirit with the view that the church is, for all practical purposes, the hierarchy of Christ that controls the sacraments. He has emphasized the priesthood as shared and the ordained ministry as representative of our common baptismal ministry. Unity and justice, especially in the form of societal transformation, are the fruit of ministry and life and a renewed church will be the ecclesial community of the poor. One may speak of a national and cultural experience of basic ecclesial communities as a reinvention of the church though in keeping with the view that the church is the visible sacrament of saving unity (*Lumen Gentium*, 9).[31] In the spirit of Boff's undertaking, the present essay tries to set out the foundation of a liberation theology that is Christological and Catholic, beginning with some biblical reflections.

For some, salvation is supernatural, otherworldly and individual. Biblically, however, the Kingdom of God embraces the transformation of our world, including its economic dimension. Its understanding of salvation does not separate the human and economic realm from the afterlife. What Israel called salvation or, more accurately, redemption was concretely a change in economic systems as the cultural etymology of the term 'redemption' suggests:

> "Throughout the land that you hold, you shall provide for the redemption of the land. If anyone of your kin falls into difficulty and sells a piece of property, then the next of kin shall come and redeem what the relative has sold. If the person has no one to redeem it, but then prospers and finds sufficient means to do so, the years since its sale shall be computed and the difference shall be refunded to the person to whom it was sold, and the property shall be returned. But if there is not sufficient means to recover it, what was sold shall remain with the purchaser until the year of jubilee; in the jubilee it shall be released, and the property shall be returned (Lev 25:24-28)".

This is the procedure laid out for the repurchase option (redemption: **ge'ullah**) by a 'redeemer' (**go'el**) of a family field that had been alienated by poverty or debt. Likewise, the Kingdom Jesus inaugurates is not 'private' or 'otherworldly'. Indeed, He describes that kingdom in terms of a city on a hill whose light cannot be hid (Mt 5:14). Or again:

> "There was not a needy person among them, for as many as owned lands or houses sold them and brought the proceeds of what was sold. They laid it at the apostles' feet, and it was distributed to each as any had need (Acts 4:34-35)."

This text, which is occasionally misunderstood as an argument against private property, in fact points to the economic impact of early Christianity. The rich invested themselves and their wealth in this new life. Work was enjoined on all Christians whereas in antiquity work was the domain of women and slaves and perhaps of certain free but poor craftsmen and farmers. This fact contributed toward a financially stable Christian community at a time when the late empire was in the midst of economic crisis. In fact, a real difficulty occurred when becoming a Christian proved economically to one's advantage. As the prevailing motivation, it threatened authentic faith and conversion of life. It also threatened the requirement to reconcile economic strength with the Lord's invitation to radical poverty. In any case it should be observed that early Christians did not think that the New Testament renounced the economic dimension of the Kingdom of God. This dimension, which finds eloquent expression in *Evangelii Nuntiandi*

(1966), is a foundational statement of the biblical relationship between political authority and liberation theology.

It is more than 35 years since the promulgation of *The Pastoral Constitution on the Church in the Modern Word* (*Gaudium et Spes*). It is an especially vital part of a tradition of Catholic and papal social thought dating to 1891. The whole document is generated by three questions: What is human existence? What is the best form of human community? What is the final meaning or value of human activity? It recognizes some fundamental economic principles. Human economic activity is called to serve the total and complete human person as an individual and as a human race. Second, human economic productivity is primarily governed by moral law and only then by laws of history and market performance. Finally, justice is the content of that moral law. As a virtue, justice moves one to more efficient production, fair recompense and protection of the family. Justice guarantees the rights of migrant workers, the right to a job and the right to security.

By contrast, certain theories take the view that economic activity is value-free and that therefore moral considerations are 'intrusions,' stumbling about where they do not belong. But the tradition of Catholic social ethics is deeply unconvinced. That tradition recognizes scarcity as arguably the fundamental problem of economics as, for example, the inability to buy food. This fact is met by justice that judges such deprivation to be evil and that establishes moral priorities between wants and scarcity. Again there is the view that checks and balances between commodities and prices achieve economic priorities 'naturally' but one misses the note of competition that has arguably (and perhaps 'unnaturally') been squeezed out of play. What value does the lack of competition serve in this value-free realm? Again, there is the view that efficiency is better served by value-free economics. In that way the greatest production is realized from the available resources. By contrast, moral considerations only make for inefficiency. But, on this view, how does one assess, for example, environmental pollution? Doesn't such a large human value belong in the efficiency equation? Or again, there is the view that ownership entails rights. But, in ethics, does the language of rights exist apart from duty and responsibility? Finally, there is the view that human behavior is characterized by 'self-interest' and that this 'selfishness' outweighs human altruism. Thus a strict construction of 'self-interest' may take the view that aiding the poor destroys the incentive to work.

The views expressed above deeply characterize modern Western Capitalism. In his classic *The Protestant Ethic and the Spirit of Capitalism*, Max Weber draws the reader's attention to the underlying view that capitalist acquisition is the virtuous fulfillment of the duties of one's calling to be hard working and frugal. This worldly asceticism glorified God and produced personal wealth as a sign of divine blessing. Weber concluded that this systematic work in a worldly calling characterized by rationality and personal asceticism deeply influenced the development of the spirit of capitalism. And it was completely unintentional! Perhaps there is more of Locke than Calvin in capitalism's family tree. In any case, recent developments around the world are clearly significant. Democracy is the key to understanding them.

Latin American liberation theology began with the rise of Fidel Castro to power in Cuba on January 8, 1959. Its pantheon of names is well known. Among them, Che Guevara in Bolivia, the election of Salvador Allende in Chile, the Sandinista experiment in Nicaragua. These were in great part opposed by military governments in Argentina, Chile, Uruguay, El Salvador and elsewhere who were responsible for truly horrific bloodbaths. But something has happened. A change has been wrought beginning perhaps with the electoral defeat of the Sandinistas on February 25, 1990. It is echoed in the collapse of International Soviet Communism. The pace of these events will only be accelerated when the postCastro era dawns.

In the minds of many, the economic injustices are still in place. How else account for the revolution that broke out some years ago in Chiapas, Mexico? Or the assassination of Colosio? In Chiapas, Bishop Ruiz was cast in the now familiar role of defender of the 20,000 displaced poor of San Cristobal de las Casas, as mediator between the Mexican federal government and the EZLN, spokesman for upwards of 40,000 Guatemalan refugees and the object of numerous death threats from coffee growers, cattlemen and landowners. How else account for the economic and social circumstances represented some years ago in the four month long siege at the residence of the Japanese ambassador to Peru? But to many these situations may now seem increasingly an anomaly.

All indications are that the future belongs to those who have abandoned the armed struggle and centralized, command economies. Politicians in the tradition of Cardenas in Mexico and da Silva in

Brazil placed well in free, democratic elections and the politics of these candidates is very much to the left. This Democratic left also counted among its ranks Jose Figueres of Costa Rica, Betancourt of Venezuela and Eduardo Frei of Chile. In fact, the superb achievement of this movement is the return of genuine democracy to lands once recently governed by right-wing military dictatorships. A utopia mentality seems gone, perhaps for good. In its place there have emerged various systems of analysis for the sake of economic progress undertaken within a culture that esteems such an undertaking and values its own institutions that are characterized by freedom and independence from government. Examples of such institutions are the church, the rule of law, freedom of the press, the discipline of the market. And these are the pre-eminent signs of a modern democracy.

It is arguable that the changes underway in economics worldwide will hasten political liberalization. This appears to have taken place, for example, in Mexico where there is now a change in the local government of the capital after quite some years. The argument is that a more open economy has helped open up its political system. Economic progress enhances the middle class and typically they practice democratic politics. In time, greater scope for choosing and a general tendency toward decentralization characterize the economic and political arenas. It is now some years since the North American Free Trade Agreement (NAFTA) was put into effect. Evaluation of its impact continues but agreements of this sort are likely to increase as regional blocs are formed. Among the first casualties of such arrangements is authoritarian government. These forces are inevitably pulling the left toward the political center. Here the shared commitment is to democracy as the best form of human polis or community because it values personal freedom and the common good. And to arrive at the common good is to find the intersection of all political authority and its foundation, together with its limitation, in the service of human rights leading to complete human potential and fulfillment.

A few conclusions are in order. This essay has espoused the view that liberation theology begins with biblical Revelation. It did not just begin a generation or so ago. Its themes as well as its justification are grounded in the biblical view of salvation as wholistic and in the relationship between divine righteousness and the classical moral virtue of justice. Such a tradition of liberation theology is welcome indeed in a world still poised anxiously along the north/south axis, with issues like defaulting on national debt, nuclear and ecological pollution, deforestation, overharvesting the seas, fresh water needs, ozone depletion and the spread of nuclear weapons. The common good, moral justice, the role of stewardship of creation and the goods contained in the notion of our Redemption all point to the validity of liberation theology in our future.

Yet there are kinds and types of liberation theology. They are to be judged on the adequacy of their analysis. Surely, continued indebtedness to a Marxist critique of consciousness and to a Marxist theory of economics will prove difficult in the present circumstances of the expanding democracy movement and economic globalization[32]. For in these current circumstances the historical Marxist failure to value human freedom and the life of the *polis* to which freedom leads is particularly unsettling. The issue is precisely the free participation of each citizen in a community characterized by shared understanding, shared decision-making, shared values and therefore a community of increasingly shared meaning regarding the human community. This appeal to the democracy of the polis does not point out an easy path. It may be it points out the only path.

ESSAY TWELVE: CHRISTOLOGY AND SPIRITUALITY

Spirituality looks to be enjoying something of a revival. Over the last few years, the major newsweeklies have devoted lead stories to the subject. Books and lectures on spirituality do very well. Clearly there is a hunger for spirituality. It is not clear how this interest squares with the broad, popular secularism of our culture. For secularism has strong intellectual moorings in a technical and scientific culture with its day-to-day commitment to practicality, efficiency and usefulness. At first glance, spirituality does not seem to share these values and indeed may seem very far removed from them. But its ability to pop up and demand attention is beyond doubt. In part, modern experience has itself shaped this phenomenon. We experience plenty, yet we are curiously empty; comfortable in our lifestyles, yet our children seem bored; possessing many 'things', yet our relationships seem insecure and weak; enjoying a great range of control over events, yet, for all that, we grow tired, old, we fall sick and die. We are successful and our education and our achievements say that we are useful, even indispensable yet we fear we shall become dependent, useless and burdensome. Perhaps we live an intensely split life, working in a world of scientific and capitalist culture yet praying desperately to God on weekends. Among the casualties of this split is the fact that we are uncomfortable even speaking of the 'purpose of life.'

But what is spirituality? Do I have to climb a mountaintop in Nepal to live a spiritual life? Must I do something equally great and heroic? By contrast, the claim set forth in this essay is very simple and straightforward: Spiritual life is the best, most basic, most integrating form of life. To advance this claim requires an answer to the question, 'what is spirituality?'

Spirituality names a profoundly human datum or phenomenon. It begins with the question, 'what am I doing when I know?' and that question generates an answer that unfolds along an ordered trajectory which may be named the achieving of higher viewpoints.[33] On the first level the answer constitutes the positivist viewpoint. It wishes to know what is in fact the case in a multiple of diverse instances. The mind proposes a law to express regularity among a set of diverse instances. The mind thus seeks a correct understanding of phenomena by means of rigorous testing and the verification of a hypothesis. The natural sciences are the paradigm of the positivist viewpoint with their concern for objective, detached, value-free, quantifiable reality expressed in knowledge as explanatory grasp with its sets of terms and relations characteristically drawn from the act of understanding itself.

In its turn, the positivist viewpoint may generate questions that it in turn cannot answer. For example, does the reality I have come to know have good or bad application? How do I distinguish good or bad? The relevance of such questions of truth and value signals the shift to the next higher viewpoint – from the positivist to the philosophic viewpoint which is devoted to articulating human interiority in terms of one's consciousness of oneself as knower and doer. Within the philosophic viewpoint new questions may arise. Having accepted the quest for truth and goodness, is there an ultimate intelligibility, a fullness of truth and goodness or is the question of ultimacy absurd? The answers intended signal a shift to the next higher viewpoint, namely, the Theist viewpoint. Within it, the quest for unrestricted explanation grasps and affirms the irreducible distinction between the contingent and the necessary, the created and the uncreated, and, within finitude, between essence and existence.

The Theist viewpoint acknowledges absolute truth and goodness, God, as the ultimate goal of the human pursuit of the true and the good. How can we share in that absolute truth and goodness? If that question is relevant, then the historical religions of the human family offer themselves as answers. In particular, the Christian viewpoint answers the question of sharing in God in terms of Jesus Christ in whom there is the perfect unity of the divine and the human. In him we share in divinity according to a specific doctrine of God as Trinity. For our participation is of such a kind that strict Monotheism cannot account for it. That explanation is to be found in the Christian doctrine of God as Holy Trinity. For within this Christian viewpoint, participation in

God is named divinization. As a fact, divinization is named Jesus Christ and as actualized by us and in us it is named Holy Spirit.

It bears repeating that the shift to higher viewpoints is accomplished not by logical deduction but by questions generated within a given viewpoint, but unanswerable within that viewpoint. Thus, a choice or invitation marks the shift from one viewpoint to another. And these viewpoints are ordered along a trajectory that, as here, can be schematically set out. Moving along these viewpoints provides the basic trajectory or look of all human spirituality. At the same time, the trajectory accounts for the meaning of human authenticity. Human authenticity is another name for spirituality. Perhaps it is also a clearer name.[34] For it names the intersection where one encounters the demand for consistency between knowing and doing and succeeds in realizing it. This would seem to validate the claim made earlier that spiritual life is the best, most basic, most integrating form of life.

These viewpoints are the product of a choice. Thus, for example, accepting the positivist viewpoint means a choice for a methodical, scientific approach to knowledge perhaps in contrast to a random and unfocused attitude. Accepting the philosophic viewpoint means that one chooses for oneself the quest for the true, the search for the good. Embracing the theist viewpoint means one chooses truth and goodness as ultimate and absolute. Finally, in accepting the Christian viewpoint, one chooses to affirm the divinization of the human in Trinitarian life. In each instance, choosing is the fruit of conversion and conversion is a decision about who I am and why I am, a decision occurring on the fourth level of conscious activity. Conversion names a movement from the unauthentic to the authentic, from fear to love. As foundational, conversion names a shift of personal horizon, a submission to the demands of the human spirit, to the transcendental precepts: be attentive, be intelligent, be reasonable, be responsible, be in love. Conversion is essentially the fruit of God's self-gift to me. As such, it is specifically named religious conversion that further expresses itself in intellectual and moral conversion. The goal of conversion is an act of faith by which I affirm the truth of this love and attach to it the highest value.[35] It is this conversion experience that underlies the choice for each successive viewpoint and the choice manifests conversion. The ordered viewpoints schematize the truth that one has fallen in love. Spirituality is the story of conversion, of the way or the ways in which I have fallen in love with God.

This account of conversion in the foundational theology of Lonergan may be helpfully filled out from a quite different perspective which Balthasar has developed.[36] Balthasar had made the case against Karl Barth that it was necessary to understand that the concept of analogy of being safeguarded the doctrine of creation. Without it, creation is drawn either into God or into nothingness. Either way it is dissolved. But analogy of being understands that the creation as such is nondivine, relative and dependent on the Creator, but that it is equally not wholly dissimilar to the Creator. This is especially true of our thinking that is affected by the fact that God thought our thinking. Thus God has created both our thinking and the reality about which we think.

Balthasar offers a fundamental insight into the nature of creation. This insight takes the form of attending to our experience of beauty. In that experience, something appears to our senses. More accurately, the senses mediate something to us. Indeed, this suggests that in the encounter with beauty there is an exterior that mediates and an interior that is mediated by the exterior. To mediate means to signify and a sensible being is constituted by sign and signified. As signified, something is expressed though not completely or exhaustively. Otherwise, what would be the reality of mediation? And, as sign, sensible being is charged with what it expresses or mediates. All created being participates in this truth that simultaneously it is both genuinely revealed and genuinely veiled. This truth constitutes the polarity of being and this polarity names what lies on the sensible surface and the depth to which it points and from which it has emerged. This polarity is characterized by mediation. And mediation is the essential meaning of truth as the unconcealedness of being. The depth dimension of truth is constituted by love or freedom that thus gives itself in the experience of beauty as the truth of being. This self-giving is directed to faith which desires to know the truth of beauty. The whole mystery of Christ, Incarnate and Revealed, takes into himself this created structure of existence specified as truth, goodness, freedom, love, within the encounter with beauty. Conversion names the experience in which one has been seized and transformed by the Glory of the Divine Love in Christ.

The foregoing account of the successively higher viewpoints situates spirituality in terms of the human datum or phenomenon of authenticity. As such it can benefit from further determinations of spirituality (and here I have especially in mind Catholic spirituality) by drawing on its history in order to deepen one's understanding and enrich the meaningfulness of the term spirituality. The balance of the essay examines several historical developments within the history of Catholic spirituality. There are three thematic sketches: first, the relationship of Scripture and Doctrine; second, how do God and the world relate?; next, the States of Life. Vignettes of well-known historical figures follow: Augustine; Francis of Assisi; Ignatius Loyola; John of the Cross; and Teresa of Avila. These sketches and vignettes are modest, tracing a few relevant points down to the sixteenth century.

The Relationship of Scripture and Doctrine

At the start of the *Metaphysics*, Aristotle observes that all human beings desire to know. This pure, unrestricted desire to know is the operator of an ascent from sense experience through understanding, judging and deciding. This ascent constitutes the normative pattern of intellectual consciousness. In it we affirm truth and make a choice for the good. And in it we can account for the shift from understanding as common sense description to understanding as explanatory grasp. Common sense description always depends on the position of the narrator. What the narrator sees, whether it stands to the left of the narrator or to the right or behind, is important, indeed necessary for the success of common sense description. By contrast, explanatory understanding generates its own sets of terms and relations. Thus, there is the famous discussion of Eddington's table. Common sense describes the table as of such a color, measurement, weight. Explanatory grasp, here in the form of atomic physics, understands the table to be made up mostly of empty space connected by wavicles of matter. One comes to grasp the distinction, for example, between describing an eclipse and explaining it. In the same way, doctrine stands to Scripture as understanding stands to the materials to be understood. Or, put differently, doctrine is the explanatory account of Scripture's common sense world. Doctrine functions by affirming Scripture as true. Doctrine thus does not in the least set Scripture aside. For that reason to speak of Doctrine as a font of Revelation alongside Scripture is not a felicitous expression since doctrine is not found **alongside** Scripture. It operates **on** Scripture. And, one notes that explanatory grasp does not use the same words as descriptive grasp. It generates its own terms and relations. How is Doctrine **in** Scripture? Not in the way that I am **in** this room. Doctrine is in Scripture in the way that explanatory grasp is **in** the materials to be understood.

A particularly instructive example of this relationship, perhaps because it takes place so early in the history of the Church, has to do with St. Athanasius.[37] By the beginning of the fourth century, Arius, a presbyter of the Church of Alexandria, collided with bishop Alexander. The cause of the collision had to do with Arius' affirmation that Jesus was not properly called divine. His argument was lean and tight. If Jesus is divine, there are two gods and if he isn't divine then lets put an end to irresponsible language. The issues represented may be expressed in the single question, 'is the Son a creature or not?'

One response to Arius took the form of appeal to Holy Scripture. But the appeal was inconclusive. For every Catholic quote, there was an Arian quote. What does the Church do when appeal to Scripture is inconclusive? The quoting of biblical texts can presumably go on without cease. In the Council of Nicea (325) Athansius lent his support to the imperial proposal that Jesus Christ is *homoousios* with the Father. What is this term? It is a philosophical term and it functions as a principle of identity. That the Son is *homoousios* with the Father means that we affirm a principle of identity between them in divinity. But, it was observed, this term is not found anywhere in Scripture. It is not **in** the bible. To this time the faith of the Church was expressed in Scriptural phrases and references. Athanasius responded that the issue was not whether the term *homoousios* was in the Scripture or not. Clearly, it isn't. The issue rather was whether *homoousios* is true or not. The term *homoousios* is true because it says that what we say of the Father the same we say of the Son except that the Son is Son and not Father. The term then entered the Creed: "We believe…in Jesus Christ…one in being (*homoousios)* with the Father…."

What did Athanasius accomplish with that word? The Catholic consciousness understands that *homoousios* stands to Scripture as explanatory grasp stands to descriptive understanding, a historical instance of the relationship between Doctrine and Scripture. Something is in the bible not as written but as understood. And on this distinction one is either a Fundamentalist or a Catholic. The historical circumstances surrounding the *homoousios* doctrine are a particularly splendid example of the deepening explanatory grasp of the relationship between Christ and Spirituality. For that relationship intends to mediate the life of Trinitarian love in its eternal self-bestowal in the crucified Jesus Christ "for us and for our salvation."

The Relationship Between God and the World

How do God and the world relate? The question opens onto two movements: Gnosticism and Monasticism. For its part, Gnosticism is a quite loose term embracing both an attitude and several technical Gnostic schools. Common to them all, however, is the view that redemption and liberation are **from** time and **from** history. This is accomplished by means of secret knowledge (hence Gnosticism). At bottom, God and the world are alien to one another and enjoy no relatedness. The spokesman for the Catholic response to Gnosticism was Irenaeus of Lyons (fl. 170-202).[38] Irenaeus developed a biblical theology based on the biblical typology of promise and fulfillment and, alternately, of image and likeness. Time and history are the developmental forces moving everything from image to likeness and from promise to fulfillment. On this biblical basis, he argued that God and the world relate dynamically and by way of analogy of being (though he never uses that venerable phrase). Implied in these notions is the fact that the finite mediates the infinite and that earthly beauty manifests the divine glory. And implied in these biblical and philosophical perspectives is a sacramental principle.

A sacramental principle expresses in a classic Catholic way the formal relationship between God and the world, the creator and His creation, divinity and humanity, infinity and finitude, nature and grace. A sacramental principle celebrates the fact that there is a real relationship between God and the world. It affirms this fact by defining and fixing that basic relationship in terms of mediation. Finitude mediates infinity, humanity mediates divinity, nature mediates grace. The invisible really gives itself in and through the visible. In this sacramental principle, the Catholic Faith 'sees' divine love, for example, in the exchange of human love in vows, in bread and wine given and received, in anointing oil, extended hands, in water and in words of forgiveness. The perspective taking shape here is of a piece with the earlier discussion of Balthasar on the nature of conversion and of the significance of our experience of the beautiful. But more than anything, the relationship between God and the world is defined with reference to the incarnation of Jesus Christ. In fact, the terms of that relationship are drawn from the Chalcedonian definition. The unity of the relationship between God and the world lies in the divine nature and will yet between the uncreated and the created there is no confusion, change, division or separation. For this reason, the Second Vatican Council taught that the unity of Christ and the Church is the *fons et origo* of the sacraments, the true sacramental principle (*Lumen Gentium*, 1). It is the mystery of Christ and the form of his existence, namely his Incarnation, that underlies and grounds the relationship between God and the world.

The ancient Church held to the view that God and the world relate as a unity because God can really be met in this world, particularly in the experience of beauty, especially the beauty of holiness. The Church held to the view that earthly beauty manifests and participates in the sacrament of divine glory. The test and verification of these remarks lay in our understanding of Redemption. For Gnosticism, Redemption was oriented away from the creation that was earmarked for destruction. For Catholic Faith, Redemption presses toward the depths of creation in the hope "…that the creation itself will be set free from its bondage to decay and will obtain the freedom of the glory of the children of God. We know that the whole creation has been groaning in labor pains until now; and not only the creation, but we ourselves … groan inwardly while we wait for adoption, the redemption of our bodies (Rom 8:21-23)."

Beauty, Sacrament, Redemption are the fruit of the struggle to answer the question how God relates to the world. Another movement that in its way attended to the relationship between God and the world was monasticism. In particular, monasticism reshaped the question of that relationship by asking 'what does knowing God look like?'

The monastic response to its own question was contained in the word contemplation or the condition of being illumined by divine truth. This gave rise to another question, namely, how does one contemplate and know God? The question sensed that Platonic contemplation and Christian contemplation are not simply identical. But it took time to articulate their distinctiveness. For example, does one take a vow of virginity to mean that one strips away the multiple in the form of illusion and shadow as well as the passions for the sake of deeper self-control in order to enter upon incorruption and unchangeable life? On this view, Christ becomes a 'divine' Socrates, instructing one in the great ascent from philosophy through the Old Testament to the New

Testament of the Church. There are numerous Platonic overtones here. For example, St. Clement of Alexandria (c. fl. 220-240) seemed to hold to the view that truth is not found intertwined in the historical, the finite and contingent. It seems rather to be a kind of homeless stranger 'down here.' For Alexandrian theology, the finite is true in its own right but it is so as the static image of the eternal. There is little appreciation of the phenomenon of development such as one finds with Irenaeus. The emphasis falls on vision and illumination rather than on relationship and emotions, on ignorance and distance rather than on bondage and sin, on disclosure rather than conversion.

One hundred years on, sometime in the fourth century, there took place a stronger Christianizing of the Platonic tradition. The movement is now away from the earlier notion of contemplating the divine substance which monasticism shared very intimately with Platonism[39]. Now contemplation is directed toward the Divine Trinity and its relationships of love. Here the emphasis falls on longing for God with all its emotional qualities and textures. The direction now unfolding leads to the view that God is known only indirectly in the intellect but directly in what God does for one in the experience of forgiveness which points out the path of conversion. Here the luminaries are St. Basil of Caesarea and St. Benedict of Nursia.

It has been said that monasticism represents life with God under the archetype of simplicity inasmuch as it focuses everything on the basic relationship between the self and God. Its central role led monks and nuns to appreciate struggle and conflict in the contest with illusion and shadow. Their prayer was characterized by the request for strength against complacency, boredom and illusion. They asked for strength to be preserved from a subtle spirituality of the ego. Fundamental to this view was the monastic appropriation of the Church's liturgical, biblical and ascetic life.

Gnosticism produced in the Church the deep sense that there was indeed a real relationship between God and the world and that that relationship was intelligible in terms of an analogy that posits a similarity in the basic relationship within a greater dissimilarity. Monasticism was challenged to contemplate this analogy, first, by freeing itself from a merely 'Platonic' contemplation and, second, by Christianizing Platonic contemplation by recourse to the biblical, liturgical and ascetic framework in which one encountered the Most Holy Trinity.

The States of Life

Perfect love is a commandment. As such it includes within itself the 'counsel' of love since love is not a duty yet the wish of the beloved is a command.[40] On this basis and just now setting to one side the priesthood, the Church came to distinguish two forms or 'states' of life – the way of the commandments and the way of the counsels (or the way of perfection). These evangelical counsels of poverty, chastity and obedience were founded on the teaching and example of Christ but he did not prescribe them for everyone. There is then the universal vocation to perfect Christian love and this is extended to all the baptized but the call to an external 'state of perfection' is based entirely on the elective will of God. Both states are willed by God and are two positive forms of Christian life. Indeed, before the historical differentiation of the states of life, there existed a union of perfect love and vow. Perfect love consists in the unconditional surrender of self and its goods to God in response to the perfect love of God for us. Our response takes the form of self-surrender in love or losing one's life for the Lord's sake (e.g., Mt 10:39; 16:25; Jn 12:25). And, in turn, this 'losing' of the self takes the form of a vow (vota meaning offering or self-surrender). Thus a vow originates in love and its motivation lies in the total gift of self. A vow inheres in love itself and precedes every differentiation of the states of life. The evangelical counsels of poverty, chastity and obedience express all the goods perfect love has to offer.

On this basis we can observe that, to the extent the vows help move one from imperfect love to perfect love, they should be seen as a means to that love that transcends them. On the other hand, insofar as love is essentially the gift of self, it partakes both formally and materially of the nature of a vow. Of itself, perfect love contains both the content and the form of the vows and it gives them constantly new expression. Finally, to the extent that love as a total gift of the self is indifferent to all God asks, it is always prepared to let its general character as a vow be actualized in whatever way or state God may desire. Each one's particular state of life represents at the same time the manner in which each is to strive to fulfill one's calling or personal mission. For the ecclesial notion of mission expresses in its turn the full measure of what human existence is and fulfillment of one's mission encompasses the whole concept of human perfection. Indeed, mission replaces the concept of human perfection by its service of the glorification of the love of the Trinity that is the single and final purpose of the creation. In this activity there is contained the whole notion of our perfection and eternal happiness.

Together with mission, there is another set of relevant Biblical terms. These are vocation and election. These terms express a twofold yet undivided act of God by which the Church participates in the separation of light from darkness and in the choice of love over hate. God elects or chooses an individual or a people. By vocation, God makes his choice known to those he has elected or chosen. Vocation is the revelation of God's choice. Together election and vocation form the basis of the state of life of the believer in the Church. And the Church is the totality of those chosen and called forth (*ekklesia*). This process of separation for the sake of union reaches within the Church. It expresses itself in a 'cruciform' division between the 'state of the counsels' and the secular state on the one hand and, on the other, between the priestly state and the lay state. This distinction, which should not be pressed too strongly, may already be seen between the apostles ("Come"; "Come and See"; "Come, follow me") and others who have been healed to whom Christ says "Go"; "Go your way." Biblically, the following of Christ begins with poverty of which virginity is a part. Poverty is a gate and the great instance of self-renunciation. In this freedom, poverty leads to obedience as the heart of the following of Christ, even to the "place outside" (Heb 13:11-13).

The state of the counsels or the state of election allows one to anticipate the world to come even now in this world while the secular state embodies life in transition from this world to the world to come. In thus carrying out what is unique to each state, they express the union between them. Baptism imparts the spirit of the vows to every Christian. Baptism thus sanctifies the secular state and enables it to participate interiorly in the heart of the state of election in the forms of poverty, chastity and obedience though without an explicit severance from the world. If the elect live in the cross, the Christian in the world lives always toward the cross. Both states of life find themselves on the same sacrificial course characterized by the same common factor in their readiness for the renunciation that makes one free for love. They share a common calling to perfect love. Christ himself lived both states of life in the gospels. Up to the beginning of his public life, he lived in the secular state as a member of a human family, born and educated, obedient to his parents. His passing into the state of election is characterized by the loosening of his natural family ties (e.g., Mk 3: 31-35; Mt 12:46-50; Lk 8:19-21).

We have been speaking to this point of the lay state in its twofold character as the secular state and the state of election (religious life or the consecrated life). The second division of the Christian state of life embraces the priestly state. There is in fact a profound unity of the Christian state of life in that poverty, chastity and obedience are the inner dimensions of the Son's perfect love that, by means of these three modes, becomes a sacrificial offering and thus point to the priestly office. The call to the priesthood embraces an objective ministry in the Church and, on that basis, subsequently a way of life. By contrast, the call to the state of the counsels is a subjective way of life in imitation of Christ and subsequently an ecclesial way of life that is similar to the official, priestly ministry but lacking the distinguishing mark of that ministry. They are both expressions of the ecclesial state of election. Together they share a more excellent law of life (sacramental consecration of the priest or the taking of vows of a religious) and a tension to live that life either in priestly ministry or by observing the Rule. The priesthood is primarily a function and an office of service and a perfect unity between office and the priest himself is unattainable. That is why the priest's self-gift lies primarily in the form of humility. Indeed, the priesthood is so completely a function in service to God that God can work in a priest even should he resist. The consecrated life is not a function but an imitation of Christ in the form of life proper to the vows of poverty, chastity and obedience. Such a person represents the renunciation of the Redeemer in the Church and for the Church. In the consecrated life the gift is mutual love and God will not lead if the religious does not willingly follow.

On the basis of the positions advanced here there is a set of relationships that govern the evangelical state, the priestly state and the lay state. First, in an ascending order of increasing intensity in the following of Christ, the movement is from lay state to priestly state to evangelical state. The second relationship of the states of life ranks the priestly state as superior to the evangelical and lay states because the priestly state and office represents the full, continual presence of Christ in the Church. As such, the priestly office (and not as a way of life) demands the obedience of the evangelical state and the lay state. This obedience is in fact the sign of their own authenticity. A third form of relationship stems from the fact that the priestly and evangelical states are permanently united in the gospels before they were differentiated. They complement each other as the objective and subjective forms of the Christian grace of mission. Together they are two aspects of the one call of Christ to follow him. Indeed their differentiation is completely at the service of the totality of the one discipleship by which a model of discipleship is established for the laity. Fourth, as the evangelical state contains the surrender of the whole person to the state of the redemption, it is united in a special way with the state of Christ and acquires a normative function in regard to the priestly and lay states. Fifth, the two states of election serve the principal state of the Church, the lay state[41], which is thus enabled to practice Christian love of God and neighbor. Finally, love becomes the integrating and ultimate form of ecclesial life whereby the states of Christian life participate in each other.

Augustine

Augustine represents a radical departure from the dominant monastic and ascetical traditions that in the East were called **apatheia** and in the West were broadly associated with Roman Stoicism. In particular, the Stoic influence may be seen in their view that happiness consists in virtue and that virtue is life lived according to reason, aiming at the highest Good or the supreme Good, the **summum bonum**. This protean notion of the Good embraced lesser goods, obvious ones such as prosperity and moral goodness and ambiguous ones such as the passions and emotions. The passions could be welcome as for example in the form of zeal or devotion or unwelcome as in the case of boredom or tedium. Distinguishing between them may require recourse to the wisdom of older monks or nuns as well as a personal grounding in the literature of the ascetical life. Never distant is the pervasiveness of Platonism that tended in broad strokes to minimize the importance and relevance of the passions in order to maintain a pure, unruffled, focused vision, the product of the divine illumination of the soul. One had to get rid of all distractions.

In some ways, Augustine is an odd fellow when it comes to this ascetical tradition. To be sure, he is profoundly influènced by Platonism especially as represented in Plotinus. But the *Confessions* are in fact a dramatic break from this ascetical tradition. This work depicts the strongest emotional experiences on which and through which God operates. They have become the stuff of the spiritual life. Written between 396-400, the *Confessions* may in part have been a reply to the considerable resistance Augustine encountered on returning to North Africa and then becoming bishop. He had been a Manichee. He had led a lurid youth and then been baptized away from North Africa. Three strikes to be sure. In the *Confessions*, Augustine has written a remarkably modern work, rich in autobiographical detail and luxuriating in psychological insight regarding behavior, motivation, illusion, passion, moral impotence and sin dark in tooth and claw. His tears are real and, in the end, the reader knows the temperament of this man from rural Thagaste, a temperament scarcely amenable to **apatheia** in any form. In this cauldron where heart and reason do battle, in this agonistic context there appears the serene breakthrough to a beauty manifesting the appearance of divine mercy:

> "Late have I loved you, beauty so old and so new: late have I loved you. And see, you were within and I was in the outer world and sought you there, and in my unlovely condition I plunged into those lovely things which you made. You were with me and I was not with you. The lovely things kept me far from you, though if they did not have their existence in you, they had not existence at all. You called and cried out loud and shattered my deafness. You were radiant and resplendent, you put to flight my blindness. You were fragrant, and I drew in my breath and now pant after you. I tasted you and I feel but hunger and thirst for you. You touched me and I am set afire to attain the peace which is yours. (*Conf* X,27)"[42]

Spirituality here embraces the domain of the autobiographical, encouraging one to assess one's own experience in the light of Christ. The impetus generated here contributed to the monastic tradition of understanding personal growth through conflict. It can be especially seen in Bernard of Clairvaux's view of the architectonic structure of love. To love oneself for the sake of the self is a poor and minimal love but God meets us there. To love God for the sake of the self is the effect of what God does for us. To love God for God's sake means we love God even as we are loved by Him. And to love one's self for God's sake is to love the self that God loves. Bernard's schema represents a vigorous and generous plumbing of the human experience about which Augustine wrote in his *Confessions*.

Francis of Assisi

Sometime in 1213, Count Orlando of Chiusi gave Francis the mountain of LaVerna, in the Apennines of central Italy. This mountain remains the heart and substance of the whole Franciscan experience. Franciscan theology is rooted here in pure contemplation. A spiritual autobiography unfolds here. Francis retired there for the 'lent of St. Michael' in August, 1224. To this day the mountaintop is scarred with jagged rocks. Throughout that month-long vigil, Francis often prayed a question redolent with passion and emotion, 'Who are you, Lord, and who am I?' His question punctuates both time and the windswept silence of the mountain. Then, Francis prayed to feel in his body, his soul, his heart, both the sorrows of Christ crucified and the crucified's love for the human race. The whole composition, saint and mountaintop, is alive with passion and feeling. There is no **apatheia** here.

Equally, there is no ascent doctrine here such as pervades the Augustinian legacy in theology,[43] a kind of Augustinian Platonism. Atop LaVerna one does not hear the siren call of Diotima to ascend from sensible beauty upward to the beauty of form, to the beauty of the Good. Instead, the Seraph descends to Francis, bearing in its embrace the crucified Christ with his wounds. These emblems of the divine love are painfully impressed on Francis' own flesh so that the wounds of Christ are become the wounds of Francis – "Look at my hands and my feet; see that it is I myself (Lk 24:39)." The movement here is in quite the opposite direction to all forms of Platonism with its ascent doctrine. Here the movement is kenotic, the descent of the Word, the Trinitarian self-giving to the world.

The encounter atop LaVerna is the hermeneutic expression of Franciscan poverty that accepts Christ's love for us, reaching us in our alienation and estrangement, in our sickness. This too is the **sacrum commercium**, the great exchange whereby Christ's love is exchanged for our sins. This poverty is suffused with the beauty manifested on the mountain. It is expressed in the autobiographical bent deeply ingrained in the Franciscan tradition with its penchant for telling stories such as those collected in the *Fioretti* (the "Little Flowers"), an anthology of stories of St. Francis and the early friars. This Franciscan poverty is also joined to a tradition of Franciscan parables as, for example, the wolf of Gubbio or the Christmas crèche at Greccio.

Augustine and Francis are very different from each other. The one broods and is given to melancholy, the other is cheerful and of a sunny disposition. The one is a scholar of language and thought, the other a poet, unselfconscious, courteous and well mannered. They both loved to preach, the one preferring the epistolary tradition of Latin letters, the other gesticulating wildly with his whole existence. In their respective ways, however, they exist at the same emotional depth. With them the experience of God is vigorous and passionate. As a result, their encounter with the living God clung to them like their clothing. People could touch God in them and like a contagion the mystery passed from one person to the next.

Ignatius of Loyola

It is not commonplace to observe (and some may remain unpersuaded) that Ignatius Loyola and Martin Luther share something important. It may be said that both men gave the notion of faith new life by returning faith to human experience. For Luther, faith is justification before God, that immense reality by which we are put right with God. And faith always trusts in God who always acts **pro me**. Grace is righteousness and not condemnation. Grace and Faith are hugely liberating experiences for Luther. For Ignatius, God chooses me. God selects me and I prefer God's choice and election to my own. God's choice of me is called conversion and my preferring God's choice to my own is a matter of true discernment in faith in order to teach me just how much I do in fact prefer God. It is important at the beginning of the spiritual life to detect sin within oneself. In grace, God gives us two experiences to assist this task. One is consolation whereby the experience of love, faith, hope and joy detect as it were their opposites. The other experience is desolation whereby the experience of darkness of soul, temptation, turbulence, and turmoil detect sin within us. These elements of the experience of desolation are not themselves sins or sinful. God uses them to allow one to detect sin. The experience of consolation and desolation can lead one to the heart of Ignatian spirituality. It lies in the understanding of grace as reproducing within us the obedience of Christ to the Father by leading us to embrace obedience to the Church. Christ's consciousness of obedience to the

Father constitutes the substance and core of his mission and of that of every disciple. Ignatian mysticism speaks about '*indifferencia*' or the attitude of receiving everything from God. This is a readiness to serve and the model for this spiritual temperament of receptivity is the Virgin Mary.

The penetrating mysticism of Ignatius is associated with the place names Manresa and La Storta, with his vision of the unity of God's plan of redemption, his vision of God the Father entrusting the Society to the Son, on a sickbed his vision of the Virgin Mary's obedience. This mystical intensity finds an echo in the Spanish Carmelites John of the Cross and Teresa of Avila.

John of the Cross and Teresa of Avila

John of the Cross asks the question 'what does the experience of God look like?'[44] His memorable answer – night! There is the night of the purification of the senses. Night is a critique of desire and knowledge and when its work is done there is only room for faith and love in the experience of God. Then there is the night of the Spirit. Here the depth of illusion is replaced with a conscious act of faith in and longing for personal identity with Christ crucified. This faith trusts where God leads which is beyond the guidance of our intellectual and conceptual apparatus. Such faith is beyond our knowledge of its ways and it leads in the direction of obscurity, vacancy or nothingness. Yet this is knowledge though of a very peculiar sort and quite unlike even the strongest experience of wordless intensity. The dynamic here is a transformation of understanding into faith, of memory into hope and of will into love. And this is the formal activity of the Holy Spirit within us. This dynamism embraces 'detachment' from externals of images, places and methods in order to maintain a 'clearing' for God lest one impede the divine operations within the self. At the end, there is a union that is characterized as a being bathed in new light. It is a species of joy and knowledge and it is expressed in a daily attitude of seeing and understanding the world as God's creation. Indeed to know creatures in this contemplative way is to know God.

By contrast with John, Teresa of Avila is wonderfully sensate. She was strongly drawn to the veneration of Christ as the '*ecce homo*.' Her depiction of her earlier spiritual life as a contest of 'two wills' evokes the drama of Augustine's *Confessions* to which she was devoted.

In fact, he remained a kind of role model for her even in the richly luxuriant sensuality of his youth. A well-known example of this sensate quality may be seen in her discourse about prayer in terms of the image of water. Water in a bucket represented discursive meditation. In the form of a water wheel, it represented affective prayer. Water as limpid springs in a fountain represented quiet and silence. The water of a drenching rain came to represent union with God.

These two Spanish Carmelites, contemporaries and friends, nevertheless reach down to our own time in the person of Edith Stein. Her reading of St. Teresa's autobiography, sometime in the summer of 1921, moved her to embrace the Catholic Faith. As a discalced Carmelite nun, she united the two Spanish Carmelites in the choice of her name, Sister Teresa Benedicta of the Cross. In the long, dark night of the war, in 1942, she produced her study of St. John of the Cross. And, in that same year, in Auschwitz, the night extinguished her. The Faith of the Catholic Church has declared her a saint with her canonization on October 11, 1998. In the words of her confrere John of the Cross, she is now bathed in new light.

The burden of this essay has gone to make the claim that spirituality is preeminently a foundational human datum. It is not an epiphenomenon. Spirituality is implicated at the depth of consciousness where one apprehends oneself as a knower and doer, as a lover. Spirituality, the claim goes, is indispensable to authenticity – to affirming it intelligently and to achieving it. In the spirit of the schema of the higher viewpoints, the essay has examined the history of spirituality in order to fill out somewhat its theoretical account of spirituality. Among the results one notes that the relationship between Scripture and Doctrine is illumined by setting it within intellectual consciousness and specifically within the distinction of human understanding as common sense description and explanatory grasp. Sccond, this examination of some points in the history of spirituality brought to light the tradition's affirmation of a real relationship between God and the world. Specifically, that affirmation is expressed both in our commitment to sacramental mystery and in our formal faith in Jesus Christ as the Incarnate Word. It also means that the monastic ethos of prayer and vigil rests on this real relationship of grace in which God and the self are brought together. The theology of the saints provides numerous examples of this relationship of grace. In the saints, one identifies sin, flesh and blood conversion, struggle, Christ crucified. Always there is the desire to experience union precisely with Christ crucified. Among the saints one finds a penetrating grasp that illumines the pattern of grace within us. And, overall, there is the palpable sense of intensity of the kind that attends what we most value.

ESSAY THIRTEEN: CHRISTOLOGY AND CONTEMPLATIVE PRAYER

The object of contemplative prayer is God and the Word of God in whom we encounter the salvation of God. By hearing, seeing and touching Jesus of Nazareth, in Holy Scripture (Lk 24:32; Jn 5:39), we come to know the eternal Word of Life who is with God and who is God.[45] Some have rightly referred to this as the scandal of particularity. Can the absolute and infinite God manifest himself in a human life? In this human life? Does it not demean the deity by making the deity into a worldly image, an idol? But Scripture does not give ground. The advent of the Word made flesh connects the Old and New Testaments and the Church awaits his return. Christian contemplation attends to the Word as the one who has come, who comes and who shall come.

When contemplative prayer attends to Christ's conversations in the Gospels we are reminded that prayer is very like human conversation. But it is God who initiates this conversation and who gives it historical breadth and depth. A particularly good example of this Scriptural conversation has to do with the Samaritan woman (Jn 4:1-42). Christ invites her to confess her sins as part of that conversation that clearly takes place within one's own intimate space – "Listen to him. (e.g., Mt 17:5)." This conversation is conducted within the flesh and blood both of the Lord and ourselves. It is thus eucharistic and concrete. The conversation leads to obedience. Accordingly this contemplation is integral to the Christian life and constitutes one as a "Hearer of the Word" and a "Doer of the Word" (Jn 8:31-32). Mary is the exemplar and pattern for contemplating the Word. Because the Virgin listens (obediently) to the Word of God she becomes the Mother of the Word and the place of the Word's embodiment.

The Word to which contemplation attends manifests Himself as truth. Faith alone affirms this truth in terms of life and love that is faithful and self-distributing. There is no other relationship between God and the world. No other access lies open to us. Indeed, this word about love affects consciousness by reshaping the ways we attend, understand and take decisions. This new consciousness embraces a fresh openness about things. It goes on to embrace renunciation as enrichment and death in terms of eternal life. To find oneself lost and guilty is equally the act by which we cast ourselves into the arms of Eternal Mercy and know ourselves saved. Our own finite existence feels stretched within this boundless love and there it receives its value as chosen and loved by God.

These manifestations of grace are often a source of joy and surprise to the contemplative. They are the heady stuff of St. Paul's idiom: "For those whom he foreknew he also predestined to be conformed to the image of his Son … and those whom he predestined he also called; and those whom he called he also justified; and those whom he justified he also glorified (Rom 8:29-30)." In this contemplation of the Word, the Father has blessed us in Christ with every spiritual blessing. An initial form of this blessing lies in the quality of *parrhesia* that is a kind of "complete speaking" in which the contemplative makes known the wonders of the divine nature and activity. In the form of confidence, *parrhesia* refers to our free and childlike approach to the Father, our right to his presence and to his attention: "Father, I desire that those also, whom you have given me, may be with me where I am … (Jn 17: 24)." And again: "On that day you will ask in my name. I do not say to you that I will ask the Father on your behalf; for the Father himself loves you … (Jn 16:26)." The truth of the Father's love is given us as a 'good conscience', the confidence to enter the sanctuary (Heb 10: 19). This peace with God in a good conscience is such a grace that we often do not know what is happening to us. Indeed our own conscience may accuse us but our defense is put forward by our "advocate with the Father, Jesus Christ the righteous (1Jn 2:1)." Thus our lack of peace at the psychological and ethical levels cannot prevail against the greater peace which is ours through grace: "And by this we … reassure our hearts before him whenever our hearts condemn us; for God is greater than our hearts, and he knows everything (1Jn 3:19-20)."

The contemplative sees visible in Christ the drama of God's love for us and the value God has set by his creation. On this basis the contemplative receives a mission to become this form of Christ who is our peace and reconciliation. With firm and intense tutelage, the Spirit directs the contemplative to the self-giving of Christ – in his eucharistic flesh and blood unto eternal life (Jn 6:54), in the surrender of his life for the sheep (Jn 10:17,28), in the surrender of his inmost spirit (Jn 19: 30), in the shedding of water and blood from his opened side (Jn 19: 34), in breathing his spirit on them in the upper room (Jn 20:22). In this activity the contemplative is aware that the Spirit brings the Son to us. The Spirit has already prepared us to receive him. Mary's vocation has already exhibited this truth.

The Spirit alone knows the hidden things of God, searching everything, even the depths of God that no eye has seen nor ear heard. He begets the mind of Christ within us and imparts his own Wisdom (1Cor 2:2-16) for our contemplation. In the Spirit one knows how unsearchable are God's judgments, how inscrutable his ways. Yet always the Spirit from God "confesses that Jesus Christ has come in the flesh…(1Jn 4:2)." The Spirit thus leads the contemplative to plumb the mystery of the triune, human-divine and ecclesial life. The Spirit dwells in us in a manner analogous to the indwelling of the Spirit in the Father and the Son, in the unity of love. Therefore the possibility of contemplation is founded entirely on the doctrine of the Holy Trinity.

The contemplative exercises an ecclesial dimension in being 'virgin-mother' of the Word. Despite concrete circumstances of location, the contemplative is not so much a solitary but one 'expanded' to the nature of the Church as virgin-mother. Thus the contemplative may mediate a wisdom to be received by another – an insight into life or tragedy or suffering, perhaps a gift of discernment or praise. Here too the contemplative may define a personal vocation in terms of a call to develop an inner sense of solitude. There one attends to God's activity *pro me* and to the fact that God has chosen me to attend to the Word and be faithful to Him.

It is one thing to talk about contemplation and another thing to do it. Yet St. Paul says we do not know how to pray as we ought. So one observes that contemplative prayer is subsumed into the prayer of the Church whose prayer is subsumed into the Son who is in the presence of the Father. In this prayer, the Father's will is done on earth as it is in heaven. This makes for a great community of 'Yes' to the Father's Will. For this reason, contemplation is oriented toward the Kingdom of God as the deepest reality and the contemplative wishes to be open before this reality. This Kingdom is more the fruit of such contemplation than the product of any action. In manifesting the hidden depths of God, the Spirit manifests the divine majesty and so there is a quite close connection between contemplation and the liturgy that is the Church's service of selfless praise to God. In particular, the liturgy of the Word is a contemplative action both in hearing the Word and preaching it. But contemplation also characterizes the liturgy of the eucharist, recalling intelligently the Lord's Passion, Death and Resurrection and entering into communion with God.

In the context of Word, salvation history and liturgy, the contemplative is profoundly free in one's communion with the Word. This Word is addressed to an individual in an action that no rule may externally restrict. The contemplative recognizes that nothing is as free as love. One is keen therefore not to allow freedom to collapse into a new slavery of selfishness or manipulation. But love is free if it is selfless and selfless love foregoes pleasure, advantage and independence for the sake of the beloved. This outlines a path of purification and testing. Love is deepened in the fire of renunciation even as love desires the presence of the beloved Word. As Incarnate, the Word will summon our senses and imagination to behold him perhaps especially in the gospel portraits of him. As humble, Christ's love is connected with the earth. This humble love of the human Christ conducts the contemplative to the Christ who is raised and exalted, sovereign over the cosmos and over death and in whom the contemplative participates.

In this activity the contemplative wishes to be alert, taking everything that proceeds from the mouth of the Word. Still, over time, contemplation extends to the prayer of quiet with its intensity and intuition in preference to discursive thinking and praying. In all this, contemplation expresses the supreme law of the freedom of the children of God. It tends to curve along the arc of love. It does not get stuck in the intellect for all seeing and hearing must result in touching (1Jn 1:1) and in getting close to God. Contemplation stands before the mystery of Christ. It does not 'solve' the mystery nor put it all together in a 'system.' Anyone who prays simply in love, willing to obey the Word, can be sure that the self will be taken up in God's truth. The self will be known by God and God will be known in faith. For the goal of contemplation is not speculation but adoration.

Christian contemplative prayer understands that the Word transforms the world. First, the Word transforms normal human existence. In its several stages and conditions the contemplative has a picture in which one sees the revelation of eternal, triune love. This is properly a sacramental mystery. Thus, the Incarnate Word enables youth, adulthood, waking, sleeping, solitude, the seasons, feasts and routines to be experiences of God. What is eternally true and valid finds expression in Christ and in the stages and conditions of his life that are identical to our own. Heaven is translated into time and time into eternity.

Second, there is the transformation from death to resurrection. It is so radical that only the power of the Father controls it (Eph 1: 18-21). In the contemplative, the passage is from the old man to the new, from the wages of sin to reconciliation. The descent into hell is behind us in our Baptism (Rom 6:3ff) so that the creation passes over into a new creation. Yet we follow the Lord in his descent and so we undergo a death and a darkness together with him. We live even now the often difficult passage from the old to the new in our experience of weariness, failure and hatred. While the passage is gradual, the victory of the cross is once-for-all. The Lord's death and resurrection lies at the center of this transformation.

Third, the Spirit manifests the truth of Christ in the faith and formulations of the Church. It is against the temper of faith to search behind the Church's faith to a presumed pure, objective, historically grounded Christ. For the Church is the medium of being as the guardian of God's sacraments. As the medium of knowledge, the Church announces to all the meaning of the world's reconciliation with God. In this the Church is Christ's body and, by his promise, the Spirit leads her into all truth. As the medium of love, the Spirit instructs the Church to understand the life of Christ as that of the love of neighbor. This last transformation of the Word is the most important and the goal of the others. Christ is the brother in all brothers and sisters, the divine neighbor in all neighbors. The neighbor is accordingly the 'sacrament of Christ.'

Balthasar has developed an integrated theological account of contemplation. It has particular ecumenical strength. He develops his understanding of contemplation as an encounter with the Word of God in Holy Scripture and as the fruit of God's grace where contemplation is characterized in terms of Faith and obedience. In grace, God has taken the initiative both in the contemplative conversation and in its sets of terms and relations. So far from being an eccentric activity, contemplation is in rhythm with the liturgy of the Church and with her sacramental life. At the same time the deepest experiences of the contemplative are illumined in terms of divine love, freedom, confidence and conversion. Finally, Balthasar has set contemplation within a Trinitarian framework where the Spirit begets in the contemplative the desire to do the Father's will on earth as it is in heaven. In this the Spirit begets in the contemplative the mind of Christ that in everything attends the Father and rejoices in His gift of the Kingdom of heaven.

ESSAY FOURTEEN: CHRISTOLOGY AND ETHICS

In Book Six of the *Metaphysics* Aristotle taught that philosophy was composed of the theoretical, the practical and the poetical. Practical philosophy embraces what we more commonly call ethics together with politics to which ethics is closely aligned. The central question of practical philosophy touches on the nature of the good and to it Aristotle returns in the opening parts of the *Nicomachean Ethics.*

The good is that at which all things aim – every art, every rational inquiry, indeed every action and purpose. As there are various arts, sciences and actions, so there are various ends at which they aim. One end, however, seems desired for its own sake and this end is properly the good or the supreme good. Yet the good is not a common idea or unity. In fact, the good is concrete and practical so that the question becomes 'what is the good in each of its instances?' All else is done for the sake of the good and the highest good is something final. What answers to this description of the good?

The short answer is happiness that is always desired for its own sake and not as a means to something else. Happiness is an activity of the soul in accordance with both reason and virtue over a lifetime. Yet the happiness that refers to one's whole life does not really consist in virtue since virtue pertains to particular states and actions. Happiness consists not in virtue but in the habitual striving (*arexis*) that leads to moral knowledge. Yet happiness and virtue are closely related since it is virtue that chooses what the moral striving of happiness desires. What emerges here is the identity of happiness with the human good. As our final end, happiness is also our final good. What about this final end? Reason is the specific human activity in which our final end consists and human excellence lies in the right and able exercise of reason. In the activity of identifying the good and choosing it, the specific virtue is practical reason (*phronesis*) and its specific activity is deliberation. Deliberation, in turn, names a process of choosing or deciding for the good. Deliberation understands alternatives and decides among them.

There is something deeply humane in this statement of practical philosophy. Human moral activity is not a matter of applying previous and prescribed principles but of understanding circumstances and possessing the knowledge that applies rules to choices. It may be said that Ethics is the story of the virtue of *phronesis*. Ethics therefore deals with the good and with deliberation. Wise deliberation is the principal function of the person who has practical wisdom (*phronesis*). Practical wisdom does not formulate general principles or even deduce what should be done. It is the ability to act so that principle will take concrete form. As such, practical wisdom is the keystone of all the virtues since the significance of virtue lies precisely in its being made concrete.

Aristotle taught the intelligibility and unity of being. The goodness of being, however, required that he consider the activities of happiness, virtue, deliberation and, particularly, the virtue of *phronesis* or practical wisdom. These are components of moral knowledge. Such, in brief, is Aristotle's contribution to rational, philosophical ethics. The view of ethics set out here is cogent and complete. One may ask, what makes rational Ethics, such as Aristotle's, to be also Christian Ethics? What does the word 'Christian' add to rational, philosophical ethics? For, to this point, 'do not even the Gentiles do the same (Mt 5: 47)?' Or, in terms of the title of the present essay, what difference does Christology make to Ethics? Would the difference be found in the way each answers the question 'And who is my neighbor (Lk 10:29)?" In fact, this question of Christian Ethics is the substance of the argument between Augustine and Pelagius.

Pelagius saw that the moral philosophy of the classical age, embracing Stoicism in addition to Aristotle, was benevolent and comprehensive. Nature gives each of us the stuff of the moral life that issues in moral reasoning, habit, virtue and deliberation. These in turn produce moral knowledge. Arguably, the centerpiece of classical moral philosophy is virtue understood as an excellence of our human nature. As such, virtue is not strictly inborn but is preceded by deliberation and itself chooses the good in some form. The polished and integral account of the good that classical moral philosophy represents has no clear and intelligible place for 'grace' within it. And surely it is grace or something very like it that makes ethics Christian. Since virtue is a free human achievement, there is no need for grace. We may think of grace as a coach who encourages one to exercise one's capacity for choosing the good. Moral life is thus a matter of a vigorous exercise of the will and, on Pelagius' view, all the conditions of moral success are provided by nature, Scripture and baptism by which one follows Christ's example. Moral failure pointed to moral slackness and moral failure was met with moral exhortation on the analogy of the coach. At the end of the day, Pelagius held that the notion of free will and the notion of the necessity of grace to do good were irreconcilable. Nature is coextensive with human existence and therefore whole and entire. What more could grace add to it? One can extend the logic here. If grace exists, it is unnecessary. If necessary, then grace is the Law, or knowledge of the Law, or Nature, or Free Will, or Remission of Sins, or given according to merit. But none of these in fact is grace.[46]

No one seems to have frustrated Augustine quite like Pelagius. Perhaps it was that Pelagius' view of grace could not at all account for Augustine's own conversion and the mystery of grace it revealed. For Augustine, there could be no question but that grace was utterly necessary for salvation. But, one can hear Pelagius say, if grace is necessary, in what sense am I free? Augustine went on to draw a helpful distinction. He allowed that the human will is created free but it is not always good. Grace gives free will the power to choose the good. The Scholastics will say that grace operates on a bad will to make it a good will and it cooperates with a good will to give it good performance so that both a good will and a good performance are due to grace.

The mention of Scholasticism invites us to consider a development in the medieval theology of grace. It begins with a question. What grace does an infant receive in baptism since the infant is incapable of performing an act? The answer took this form, viz., that the infant receives grace as a *habitus* or disposition or orientation. Grace as a *habitus* eliminated 'works righteousness' by making grace causal in the performance of good works. For good works are the fruit of grace in us that gives us this disposition or orientation to good works. Grace as a *habitus* emphasized the effectiveness of divine love that produces a real, entitative change in us, a real transformation at the level of our orientation and disposition. This was the created effect of the real indwelling presence of the Trinitarian God as grace. Finally, grace as *habitus* makes human acts meritorious because the *habitus* is itself a human orientation or disposition.

These consequences of the teaching on grace as a *habitus* are significant chiefly for their failure to carry the day in the late medieval period. Nominalism had understood the relationship between the divine and the human as unbridgeable except by Faith. Reason was limited to its function within creation. What we have been describing as *habitus* or created grace 'fell' to the side of creation and our human nature with nothing to do with grace. Indeed, Luther understood created grace as a species of Pelagianism. There is not a little irony here inasmuch as created grace or *habitus* was put forward in part to counter Pelagian tendencies. Still, with Martin Luther, the gap between the created and the uncreated was unbridgeable except by Faith alone, Scripture alone, Grace alone. These historical perspectives are relevant to the contemporary question of Ethics as Christian.

Protestant dialectical theology begins with Scripture. Jesus is God's 'yes' to us. Jesus has already done what we are to do. As Lord, Jesus requires what is to be done and he empowers us to do what he requires. Christian Ethics in this tradition is Christocentric. All is under Christ's Lordship and Christian Ethics knows of the constant struggle to conform to the reality of Christ. For Barth, grace is constitutive of freedom so that, in Christ, we are free to obey God's Word. Faith in Christ removes the whole supposition of all self-centered ethics, namely, that goodness or moral value or rightness has its source in the character of the human being. In this sense, Christ frees us from "ethics." From this point of departure, Barth holds that all criteria of moral guidance must be derived from Christ or from the implications of his being the center of life, from his sovereignty. Barth distinguishes casuistic ethics, which is misguided, and practical casuistry that in the process of reflection offers some basis of guidance. The Scripture becomes a source of insight into the processes of practical casuistry or moral reflection, yielding analogies though not rules or ethical universals. It is Faith in Christ that makes Ethics Christian. This Faith makes its greatest difference in the basic attitude or disposition of the moral human being. Faith in Christ frees one from prescriptive ethics in favor of openness to the world and its infinite possibility. This relationship to Christ in obedience is then expressed in the ethical activity of assembling facts, analyzing them and making a judgment.[47]

Bultmann is another proponent of Christian Ethics in the tradition of Protestant dialectical theology. God's gift in Christ is one of radical freedom for the present[48] and future. In this project, there is no Christian morality nor Christian virtue. Christians belong now to the new age which is a life given in hope. In hope and love the Christian obeys God's demands. The self is essentially 'unstructured', existing in discontinuous moments of obedience rather than as a character with qualities of life that bridge the momentary. Grace frees and commands this self. It does not affect habits or consciousness. The order of creation only locates the human being in a concrete place of obedience. Bultmann's ethic does not admit prescriptive ethics. It is neither a social ethic nor a political one. For Bultmann, at the end of the day, the significance of Christ for the moral life is not to give a pattern to moral activity nor to be the source of moral teaching but to provide the freedom and openness to obey the command of God in the present. In that sense perhaps it lays claim to being a critical ethic.

Is this an adequate account of ethics as Christian? If Scripture and Revelation are discontinuous with human wisdom or philosophy, then there can be no connection between Christian Ethics and rational, philosophical ethics. The difficulty with the dialectical tradition of Barth and Bultmann may lie not so much in its account of ethics as in its understanding of Revelation which alone bridges the gap between God and the creation. One alternative to these views understands that God creates what is nondivine, relative and dependent but, equally, what is not wholly dissimilar to the creator. Our thinking too must exhibit the truth that God created our thinking. Indeed God thought our thinking. So it may be that the dialectical understanding of Revelation is inadequate. It does not go far enough. What is more, while Christian Ethics in this tradition is much described as Christian it is little enough described as ethics. How can it be ethics without some account of human psychology, of the formation of character, the nature of human acts, the cause, meaning and nature of virtue? Can these be dismissed as unworthy of Christian Ethics or as superseded by appealing to the *kerygma* of the Lordship of Christ? Put differently, sometimes the wrong question is posed in the form 'what must a Christian do which a rational nonChristian presumably would not do?' The proper question asks why a moral agent makes a judgment as to the good to be done and decides to do it. This question 'why' brings a Christian to the consideration of the kind of person he or she is 'in Christ' and only then to what is to be done.

In *Insight*, Lonergan has set out a notion of ethics that makes the case that for rational ethics to be complete and integral it must be a religious ethic. He begins by distinguishing the intelligible and the good:

> "As being is intelligible and one, so also it is good. But while the intelligibility and unity of being follow spontaneously from the fact that being is whatever is to be grasped intelligently and affirmed reasonably, the goodness of being comes to light only by considering the extension of intellectual activity that we name deliberation and decision, choice and will."[49]

These remarks indicate that Lonergan conceives the possibility of ethics along the same lines as metaphysics. There are several levels of the good. The good is the object of desire. The unique human desire is the detached, disinterested, unrestricted desire to know. This unique desire grasps in recurring desires an intelligibility of the good of order. The good of order embraces society, the economy and the institution of the family. The good of order is not the object of any single desire but is itself dynamic, possessing its own normative line of development that is seen in human moral knowledge.

In fact, what the good is and how it may be known is absolutely a human question. The good is the object of human desire for the good's own sake. As order, the good is social and as social it involves both the individual and the communal.[50] The good of order then is radically subject to the human including human bias, egoism and deviation from the good of order. The good of value exposes these failings. As it is joined to the good of order at the level of reflection and judgment, deliberation and choice, the good of value requires some account of the notion of the Will.

The Will is an intellectual or spiritual appetite dealing with objects presented by the intellect. In addition to this bare capacity, there is habitual inclination which constitutes either the willingness or the unwillingness that characterizes a person's disposition in making decisions or choices. The 'habit' is one's 'willingness.' This willing is rational and therefore moral. The intellect grasps not only facts but practical possibilities. Here, a single consciousness grounds knowing and doing and, from this identity of consciousness, there arises the demand for personal consistency between knowing and doing. And, if knowing itself is subject to distortion, how much more is this the case when knowing is extended beyond facts to human living?

Value is the good as the possible object of rational choice. As there are different divisions of value, so there is a need for moral precepts or ethical principles. The root of ethics, however, does not lie in propositions or judgments, but in the dynamism of rational self-consciousness. On this view, moral precepts or ethical principles are based not on propositions or judgments, but on human persons. Indeed, the radical openness of the human spirit is the *fons et origo* of the transcendental precepts that are immanent and operative in the human spirit. As precepts they may be named: be attentive, be intelligent, be reasonable, be responsible.

The Will is inseparable from freedom and freedom invites to some account of practical knowledge – with something to be done and the reasons for doing it. As with all knowledge, practical knowledge depends on a practical insight, namely, what ought to be done. It depends on practical reflection since rational self-consciousness demands both knowledge of what one proposes to do and the reasons for doing it. Practical reflection ends with a decision in order that the proposed action remain no longer a possibility. In this strict contingency of intelligent grasp, rational reflection and morally guided Will, freedom emerges. So freedom emerges in the order of spirit and it is particularly evident in making decisions. It excludes necessity. The measure of the freedom of an act is also the measure of the responsibility of the doer. The human person is essentially free inasmuch as possible courses of action are grasped by practical insight, motivated by reflection and executed by decision. Clearly, however, while the human person is essentially free the matter is different regarding effective freedom. As Lonergan observes, one may be essentially free, but not effectively free, to give up smoking.

Effective freedom implies conditions of limitations. These may derive from the environment, from psychological factors, from an absence of virtue. Effective freedom must therefore be won and enlarged. It is proportionate to full intellectual and volitional development and, as this is never completely achieved, the proportion becomes the measure of moral impotence. Moral impotence is an invitation to development, to learning from mistakes. Yet, at the same time, human bias and egoism render sustained development problematic. Life becomes tense and confused. There are contrary views of the good. The problem of moral impotence is radical and situated in the very dynamic structure of cognitional, volitional and social activity. And, because this structure is a potentiality in process of development, the problem of moral impotence is permanent and more profound than the ability of the arts and sciences to rectify. The problem of moral impotence lies in the very dimensions of human history. It is a problem of liberation so permanent and radical, so independent of philosophy, the arts or sciences, as to raise formally the question of the ultimate finality of human life.

Some conclusions are in order. Lonergan has presented a system of rational ethics that is essentially open and complete. It is complete in that it accounts for the ingredients necessary to any cohesive account of ethics. In this connection, one may note that, in his account of the good of order, Lonergan has retrieved the ethical tradition of the common good and in his account of the transcendental precepts he has expressed the ethical tradition of natural law. Lonergan's ethics is open both to the dynamic structure of human knowing and to the inner capacity of that dynamism to raise the question of the finality of human life. This openness as such heads in the direction of a religious ethic as an account of one's responsibility before God. Lonergan's ethics is not ashamed of the natural human ability to know the good and do it. It exalts essential human freedom but in its analysis of effective freedom a radical human incapacity is laid bare. It is here that the mystery of Christ can best be seen. God as Creator has graced nature. God as Redeemer heals the grievous wound of sin, deviation, radical incapacity. Christian ethics, understood as the grounding of the believer in Christ, is possible because a complete and open rational human ethics is possible. And this seems to confirm the claim that a rational ethic, to be complete, must also be a religious ethic.

Balthasar has also set out a Christological ethic in his meditation on the dramatic quality of Revelation that he has named Theo-Drama. "It is the history of an initiative on God's part for his world, the history of a struggle between God and the creature over the latter's meaning and salvation."[51] The point of contact between drama and Revelation lies in freedom since without it there is no dramatic action at all. The specific dramatic form of freedom within theodramatic action is the obedience of Christ that as such manifests the glory of the Father's love for the world. Christ's obedience is the highest norm of freedom and it invites all freedom to its standard and form.

Balthasar unfolds his ethics or, in his words, his theodramatic action around two principles: the Adam principle and the Christ principle.[52] Together these constitute human history. Human actions take place in a context of vertical and horizontal history and in an existence characterized by time, death, freedom, power and evil. One observes how different these terms are from those employed either by Aristotle or by Lonergan.

In the Adam principle, time and death seek each other out. Time belongs to me as finite yet it is beyond my control especially with regard to my beginning and my end. Time and death together are the structure of my "being-with" others. Death brings into view not simply the truth that the absolute irradiates the finite but the truth that the absolute has actually become finite in the Risen Christ. In him the finite is thus drawn into what is ultimate and eternal. In Jesus, God is asked 'why do you forsake me?' God's answer turns on re-creation, transfiguration, the weight of glory, the fact that former things have passed away. In Christ, death and time have returned to their obedience to God.

Death and freedom also interact. The human being is dependent on the free self-disclosure of others in order to be self-possessed. As free, this self-disclosure cannot be coerced. Similarly, the human being is dependent on God's free self-disclosure inasmuch as we are created to be receptive to absolute truth and goodness. Created freedom must recognize its creatureliness, its givenness, in order to discern and grasp itself. In that givenness, absolute freedom and its normativity is disclosed. Only in this way can created freedom be truly free. In turn, this requires the human being to acknowledge that our existence is a synthesis that yet lacks fulfillment, an oscillation that finally can only rest in God and in the divine self-disclosure.

Freedom is the most fundamental expression of human power that is itself eminently a part of the goodness of creation. But evil is closely allied to power. Power is the cause and sphere of decisions, especially ultimate ones such as the decision either for God or the demonic. This interplay requires that fundamental decisions be taken. Yet finite freedom is bi-polar in that it possesses both genuine autonomy and a real indebtedness and these are irreducible to each other. The finite spirit is conscious that it understands, possesses and loves itself, but that it has not given this self-possession to itself. It is in fact a gift from infinite freedom that thus becomes normative for finite freedom. Finite freedom must transcend itself in the direction of infinite freedom if it is to possess itself in accordance with its own truth. The genuine autonomy of finite freedom stems from the fact that its *nomos* is genuinely communicated and given to it yet it comes from the absolute and as such it is given with a view to the absolute.

Finite freedom has as its origin the identity of absolute freedom and absolute power. In its self-possession and in its choosing correctly, finite freedom becomes aware that it has an inviolable power inseparable from the absolute norm of the good. The 'good' reveals itself the moment this freedom is bestowed, drawing aside the veil to show that absolute power is identical with absolute self-giving. In this way, all ethical conduct is rooted in religion.

The primordial temptation, the original sin, is to be 'like God, knowing good and evil (Gen 3:5).' In effect, the temptation was to separate power and goodness while setting oneself up as the standard of the good and subordinating the good to one's own exercise of power. The possibility of evil arises from the polarity of human freedom. As we have seen, this freedom has been genuinely handed over and entrusted to itself and it knows this. To be self-possessed, it must acknowledge its indebtedness and in doing so, transcend itself. For the sake of acknowledging this indebtedness, the absolute good communicates itself to us in a hidden and latent manner, but the fact of the gift as perceived by finite freedom is fully illumined. In the name of its autonomy, evil denies the indebtedness of finite freedom to absolute freedom. In doing this, evil takes the form of the lie. This is the situation of original sin. It not only points out an enduring situation of the lack of grace. It also represents a profound solidarity of all human destinies in terms of suffering and death. It awaits the Christ principle.

God's action in the Christ principle is embraced by the term soteriology or atonement. It refers to a final event of reconciliation within the tradition of election and covenant. This is the content of soteriology and that tradition is historically represented in the terms exchange (*commercium*), substitution and solidarity. Solidarity is the more modern term. It has, however, labored under the tendency to express a mere social or psychological bond. Other difficulties have attended the effort to retrieve the Patristic notion of *commercium* by depriving it of its properly ontological dimension. For its part, substitution lost the Patristic sense of an exchange of divine and creaturely nature in Luther who understood it as the exchange between the sinner and Christ, the bringer of grace. The notion of solidarity must always keep in view Christ's representative or vicarious suffering so that solidarity extends as far as substitution, the exchange of divine and creaturely nature. This exchange is the dramatic element, the primal tragedy, of the scapegoat that is epitomized in Christ.[53] Its effect is to revolutionize and unmask everything. The mechanism of the scapegoat must essentially be hidden and unrecognized and this makes it profoundly ambivalent or merely fortuitous. Yet it must not be conceived in terms of repression and the unconscious. On this basis, what really takes place on the cross in reference to the Father? Human beings themselves place every 'No' on the Son as a burden that presupposes that he can bear sin for us and wills to do so. His willingness springs from the mission his Father has given him and which is rooted in his coming forth from the Father.

At the end of the day, Scripture presents soteriology under five connected motifs: (1) The Son gives himself, through God the Father, for the salvation of the world; (2) The sinless One 'changes places' with sinners; (3) Human beings are, thus, set free (or ransomed or redeemed or released); (4) Indeed, the human being is initiated into the divine life of the Trinity; (5) Thus the whole process can be seen as the result of divine love's initiative.[54] Together these motifs constitute theo-drama since here absolute freedom enters into created freedom, interacts with it and acts as created freedom. Put differently, theo-drama is here the drama of the Trinity in the 'emptying' of the Father's heart in the generation of the Son.

This drama contains and surpasses all possible drama between God and the world. It is the drama of our Redemption in which God takes possession of us – '…you are not your own (1Cor 6:19b).' And again: 'And he died for all, so that those who live might live no longer for themselves, but for him who died and was raised for them (2Cor 5:15).' We live for Christ, putting him on (Rom 13:14; Gal 3:27), having his mind (Phil 2:5). This is the air Barth breathes and in that spirit he is surely right that faith in Christ makes ethics Christian. The difficulty is that Barth has not gone far enough. Lonergan has grasped what is required to overcome the difficulties faced by dialectical theology. He expresses the view that rational ethics, to be complete and integral, must be a religious ethic. He affirms that ethics is rooted not in prescriptions and norms, but in the dynamism of rational self-consciousness. Finally, he affirms that freedom emerges in the order of spirit and is particularly evident in the decisions we take. Balthasar too illumines the nature of ethics. Freedom is the basic category of his theo-dramatics. Freedom accounts for human self-possession, for the disclosure of infinite freedom, for the ingratitude of evil both in failing to acknowledge the rootedness of freedom in infinite freedom and in separating power and goodness.

ESSAY FIFTEEN: BALTHASAR, LONERGAN AND ST. THOMAS

One of the great difficulties in dealing with these two wide-ranging and prolific authors lies in the unwelcome tendency to juxtapose them. Thus, on any given point, one says this and the other says that. I have wanted to avoid such an outcome in part by taking care to express their unity of thought and insight at different points in a number of essays. However, it has seemed best to devote a final essay to the unity of thought to be found in Lonergan and Balthasar. If the case for this unity can be made, it will go a long way toward avoiding the problem of merely juxtaposing them. One does not wish to leave the impression that these two thinkers are like two men standing next to each other in a crowded subway car. In the Introduction, I indicated my belief that the source of their unity lies in the way each reads St. Thomas Aquinas, the Common Doctor. In the present essay I should like to return to that claim.

Clearly both our authors have read deeply in St. Thomas. They have published their research in substantial and scholarly works.[55] That fact on its own suggests Thomas as a unifying factor in their thought. Still some may be struck by what they take to be the sharp difference between these two authors in the basic matter of knowledge. In particular, what place has beauty or aesthetic consciousness (such as one finds in Balthasar) in working out an account of knowing? In adequately differentiated consciousness one distinguishes, for example, aesthetic consciousness from theoretical consciousness. The former attends to beauty and creativity, its manifestations, forms, instruments and materials. The latter works out the nature of understanding as explanatory grasp that expresses itself in the sets of terms and relations such understanding generates. Philosophical problems in the area of knowledge can be met by appealing to underlying differences in cognitional theory that answers the question, 'What am I doing when I am knowing?'

Among Thomas' major achievements there is his teaching regarding *esse* (existence), its relation to essences, and the real distinction between them that is based on the real distinction between the two operations of the intellect by which they are known. For within theoretical consciousness there is a real distinction between knowledge of essences and knowledge of existence (*esse*), between understanding and judging. Thomas understands *esse*, the act of being, as the non-subsistent fullness and perfection of all reality. *Esse* does not subsist or exist in itself . *Esse* inheres only in natures or essences. Apart from them, *esse* does not subsist or exist so that *esse* is simultaneously total fullness and total nothingness. *Esse* is total fullness because existence is the act of being inasmuch as it is a being. And *Esse* is total nothingness since the notion of being apart from essence is the notion of nothing. *Esse* is the supreme 'likeness of divine goodness' which creates in knowledge, freedom and love as Scripture teaches. The *actus essendi* is God's primary, immediate and comprehensive act of creating. Thus, God is not the being of things, but their efficient, exemplary and final cause. God is thus radically removed from created being as 'Wholly Other.' This truth has often been expressed by saying that we can know that God is, but not what he is. This is the area of negative theology. Revelation and the knowledge of God that is faith do not eliminate negative theology, but in fact enhance it because, although God is manifest in the realm of *ens commune*, the divine essence does not belong to it. In the words of Holy Scripture, this is the manifestation of divine glory. This Thomistic account of essence and existence constitutes the common basis for the unity to be found in the thought of Lonergan and Balthasar.

The notion of divine glory leads to some account of the place of the *pulchrum* (beauty) in relation to *verum* and *bonum*. Thomas understood that there is a fundamental unity of the good and the beautiful, since both are based on form or the intelligibility of a thing. At the same time, however, he drew a distinction between them. The good pertains to desire since it is desired by all and is therefore an end. Beauty, on the other hand, relates to a cognitive power (*vim cognoscitivam*) since something is beautiful which pleases when seen. Here, in its relationship to a cognitive power, beauty is distinguished from goodness and drawn toward the true as *pulchritudo veritatis*, the beauty of truth. Thomas adds that the supreme beauty of human nature consists in the splendor of knowledge. This Thomistic framework is supple and, in what follows, it is possible to demonstrate in what ways it has room for both the cognitional theory of Lonergan's transcendental method and the Theological Aesthetics of Balthasar.

What am I doing when I am knowing? The basic pattern of our cognitional activity rises on the three levels of experience, understanding, and judging. Experience is the level of data, presentations, the empirical, the merely given. Understanding achieves insight into data and has an idea as its content. Understanding issues in hypotheses, theories, definitions, concepts, formulations. This is the level of thought. The possibility of insight on this level is the possibility of the enormous development of intelligence that characterizes human history. The third level yields reflective understanding which takes possession of the evidence and makes judgments which affirm that something is true or not. This is the level of rationality, reasonableness, knowledge. Beyond these, and united to them at the level of personal consistency between knowing and doing, there is the level of decision and responsibility. Here one must decide how to act on the basis of what one knows. An adequate cognitional theory objectifies this pattern in answer to the question 'What am I doing when I am knowing?' This pattern provides the fundamental notion of method. A method is a normative pattern of recurrent and related operations yielding cumulative and progressive results.[56] Indeed, this notion of method is strictly transcendental which adds to the notion of method the fact that the results envisaged are not confined categorically to some particular field or subject but regard any result that could be intended by the completely open transcendental notions. The operations identified in the basic pattern of our cognitional activity are in their distinct ways both conscious and intentional and these operations yield the transcendental notions that are comprehensive, intending every unknown, asking unlimited questions.

Thomas understood form as determining a thing in its kind or species and distinguishing it from other kinds of beings or from other species. Form or the splendor of form is the intelligibility or clarity of something. It is often specifically beautiful or radiant because it is found in the sensible by the senses. The higher or greater the form, the greater its power to unify the manifold and to relate all intelligible forms to each other. Form thus constitutes a principle of unity or intelligibility that appears in the parts it unifies even as it transcends them from within a being. Balthasar[57] will go on to say that this principle of unity is properly interior in a being, marking a polarity, more or less large, of interior and exterior, a distance that freedom measures and a self-giving that beauty manifests. When beauty is no longer understood, existence is no longer intelligible because the intellect cannot coerce human free interiority which remains free before, in, and after its manifestation. Interpersonal knowledge is thus formally determined by the authentic freedom of human persons. These elements of form, its splendor, and its self-giving in freedom are the intelligibility of existence that beauty discloses.

The position represented here is that the unity in the thought of Lonergan and Balthasar lies in their appropriation of the Thomistic teaching regarding essence and existence. On this basis, one can retrieve the basic statement of Thomas' response to the question 'What am I doing when I am knowing?' On that same basis, one can retrieve Thomas' response to the question, 'What do I know when I perform these operations?' What is known he conceived metaphysically in terms of matter and form, potency, habit and act, efficient and final causes.

The real distinction between essence and existence is a hallmark of finite being and it points toward the theological relationship of nature and grace. God has imparted something of himself to finite being in terms of an inner relationship of origin and transcendence. This relationship allows finite being to encounter the mystery of the Incarnate Son beyond every limitation that finite being experiences. This may be illustrated in terms of two Marian doctrines. In her Assumption, Mary, representing finite or created being, is received into heaven by her Son who is the heavenly one she had received on earth. This capacity of finite being to receive and be received by God constitutes human existence as *imago Trinitatis*. But it is grace that makes possible this capacity of finite being. Thus, in her Immaculate Conception, we understand that grace enjoys the priority in giving human finite existence the grace to receive grace in its fullness. I believe that the clarity and sharpness of these theological perspectives regarding the relationship of nature and grace are enhanced by the Thomistic teaching on the real distinction between essence and existence in the matter of finite being.

CONCLUSION

The Word of God has renounced the task of fashioning a Christology preferring instead to give that task to the Spirit of truth: "…he will take what is mine and declare it to you (Jn 16:14)." In this he will glorify the Son. It is fitting that this should be the final context for Christology – it is to our advantage (Jn 16:7). Thus, the Spirit makes unutterable groans within us and, unseen, illumines the relationship of the Father and the Son. He is their love, the love that has appeared in Christ. The Spirit of truth, the Advocate whom Christ sends, understands and teaches Christology. In doing this, he will guide us into all truth because he will not speak on his own, but he will declare to us whatever he hears. He will declare the things that are to come (Jn 16:13). A shift is envisioned here. It is the value of looking at Christ with pneumatic eyes even as we are accustomed to looking at the Logos with logical and philological eyes. God has revealed through the Spirit what no eye has seen nor ear heard, even the depths of God. For no one comprehends what is truly God's but the Spirit that is from God (1Cor 2:9-11). Under his tutelage a Christology takes shape 'in words not taught by human wisdom but taught by the Spirit, interpreting spiritual things to those who are spiritual (1Cor 2:13).' Without this binocular view, we are unable to attain the Christian and ecclesial dimension of Christology. As a result we are left with so many unintegrated pieces – Scripture, Tradition, Gospel, Church. We have so often been stuck here. I believe that between them our two authors achieve a binocular vision in their view of Christology inasmuch as they present us with an integrated vision of Scripture, Tradition, Gospel and Church. Yet their vision welcomes the contribution of scientific, historical and exegetical monographs.

In this Conclusion we arrive at a kind of 'Amen' (Rev 22:20) — *Si comprehendis non est Deus.* Our knowledge of God is sustained by faith and love lest it be 'puffed up' (1Cor 8:1). It is centered on the Eucharist that shapes the high Pauline doctrine of Kenosis and of being 'in Christ.' This fundamental assertion has always seemed to me to characterize our two authors. It makes reading them a theological experience. They share the fruits of their own *lectio divina.* Yet where are we at the end of this book? What do we know about this 'Son', this 'heir' who is the entirely adequate expression of God's very being (Heb 1:3)? Do I sense that I am now nearer a response to the question Christ put to the disciples regarding his identity – "Who do you say I am?" "Do you then still not understand?" (Mk 8:17) This after all is a test of all Christological reflection.

ENDNOTES

[1] Studies that combine Lonergan and Balthasar are few. I recommend Robert M. Doran, S.J., "Lonergan and Balthasar: Methodological Considerations," *Theological Studies*, 58, 1 (March, 1997), 61-84. He returns to the subject briefly in "Bernard Lonergan and the Functions of Systematic Theology," in *Theological Studies*, 59, 4 (December,1998), 569-607. Anne Hunt, "Psychological Analogy and Paschal Mystery in Trinitarian Theology," *Theological Studies*, 59, 2 (June, 1998), 197-218. In her footnote 4, she refers to Hilary A. Mooney, *The Liberation of Consciousness: Bernard Lonergan's Theological Foundations in Dialogue with the Theological Aesthetics of Hans Urs von Balthasar,* Frankfurter Theologische Studien (Frankfurt: Josef Knecht, 1992). Finally, I note John D. Dadosky, "The Dialectic of Religious Identity: Lonergan and Balthasar," Theological Studies, 60, 1 (March,1999), 31-52.

[2] See my "Some Methods of Interpretation in St. Irenaeus," *Vetera Christianorum*, 30 (1993), 123-132.

[3] Some relevant texts: *De Somniis* I, 13; *De Abrahamo* 15; *De Specialibus Legibus* 39 and *De Victimis* 5.

[4] Essay Eight; "Objections and Difficulties With 'Chalcedonian' Christology."

[5] In the last several paragraphs I have hewn very closely to Lonergan's "Christology Today: Methodological Reflections," *Le Christ hier, aujourd'hui, et demain.* R. Laflamme and M. Gervais (eds). Quebec: Les Presses de l'Universite Laval, 1976, 45-65.

[6] See, for example, Raymond E. Brown, S.S., *The Death of the Messiah*, I and II, (New York: Doubleday, 1994), I, 325-327; 462-547;

[7] Hans Urs Von Balthasar, *Explorations in Theology II: Spouse of the Word,* (San Francisco: Ignatius Press, 1991), "Fides Christi", 43.

[8] A thoughtful meditation on Paul may be found in Hans Urs Von Balthasar, *You Have Words of Eternal Life,* (San Francisco: Ignatius Press, 1991), 237-238 with the title "I Will Show Him." This book of meditations has much to commend it.

[9] This essay has drawn substantially on Balthasar's theology of the Church. I refer the reader to his *Theodrama. Theological Dramatic Theory. III. Dramatis Personae: Persons in Christ,* (San Francisco: Ignatius Press, 1992) and his *Explorations in Theology II: Spouse of the Word,* 289-298. And see Joseph Fessio, S.J. *The Origin of the Church in Christ's Kenosis: The Ontological Structure of the Church in the Ecclesiology of Hans Urs Von Balthasar*, (Dissertation: University of Regensburg, 1974).

[10] "...'What are you looking for?' They said to him, 'Rabbi...where are you staying?' He said to them, 'Come and see' (Jn 1:38-39)."

[11] The theology of the three Marys is set out in *Explorations in Theology, III: Creator Spirit*, "The Mass, A Sacrifice of the Church?" (San Francisco: Ignatius Press, 1993), 224-228 or in *The Von Balthasar Reader*, Medard Kehl, Werner Loser (eds), (New York: Crossroad, 1982), "Indifference in the Gospel of John," 322-325. A related and equally fundamental point is Balthasar's meditation on the relationship between Peter and John the Evangelist in terms of the Church of Office and the Church of Love. See his *Mysterium Paschale*, (Edinburgh: T&T Clark, 1990), 258-261.

[12] In this connection the reader may wish to consult Essay Ten on feminism and Essay Eleven on the liberation of peoples. Balthasar himself provides a thorough and sobering historical overview of the Church as sinful in *Explorations in Theology II: Spouse of the Word*, "Casta Meretrix," (San Francisco: Ignatius Press, 1991), pp 193-288.

[13] See also V. Bradley Lewis, "Globalization and the Eclipse of Natural Right: What We Might Learn From Plato And The Other Greeks," in *Communio*, 27 (Fall 2000), 431-463. Lewis has developed his thoughts in connection with globalization and so may be read also in connection with Essay Eleven "Christology and the Liberation of Peoples."

[14] See Essay Eight, "Objections and Difficulties with Chalcedonian Christology."

[15] In a number of his works, Lonergan touched on the shift from a classicist to a historicist worldview. I recommend his *A Second Collection*, W.F.J. Ryan and B.J. Tyrrell (eds), (London: Darton, Longman & Todd, 1974; Philadelphia: Westminster, 1975), "The Transition from a Classicist World-View to Historical Mindedness," 1-9. On the notion of 'paideia' see Werner Jaeger, *Early Christianity and Greek Paideia,* (London, Oxford, New York: Oxford University Press, 1969). On Irenaeus, see Hans Urs Von Balthasar, *The Glory of the Lord. A Theological Aesthetics, II: Studies in Theological Style: Clerical Styles* (San Francisco: Ignatius Press, New York: Crossroad, 1984), 31-94.

[16] Eusebius, *Ecclesiastical History*, Books IX, X (Cambridge: Harvard University Press, 1973), II.

[17] The major work that lies behind the whole essay is Bernard Lonergan's, *The Way to Nicea*. The Dialectical Development of Trinitarian Theology. Conn O'Donovan (transl), (London: Darton Longman & Todd, 1976). In an enormous field of Patristic scholarship, see Aloys Grillmeier, S.J., *Christ in Christian Tradition*, I, From the Apostolic age to Chalcedon (451), John Bowden (transl), (Atlanta: John Knox Press, 1975). Finally, an old, slightly dated favorite, G.L. Prestige, *Fathers And Heretics*, (London: SPCK, 1940), "Athanasius: or, The Unity of God", 67-93.

[18] For the whole definition and for a helpful context, see *Documents of the Christian Church*, Henry Bettenson (ed), (London: Oxford University Press, 1967), 51-52.

[19] Bruno Snell, *The Discovery of the Mind*. The Greek Origins of European Thought. T.G. Rosenmeyer (transl), (Cambridge: Harvard University Press, 1953), Introduction, v-xii.

[20] Some of the points to be found in this essay are treated at greater length in Matthew Lamb, *History, Method and Theology. A Dialectical Comparison of Wilhelm Dilthey's Critique of Historical Reason and Bernard Lonergan's Meta-Methodology,* (Missoula: Scholars Press, 1978). Lonergan himself treats these points in *Method in Theology*, (New York: Herder and Herder, 1972), chiefly under "History", 175-196, under "Dialectic", 235-266, and under "Foundations", 267-293. While the essay has adhered closely to Lonergan, Balthasar shares the spirit of Lonergan's remarks regarding Scholasticism. In brief, while the patristic period could not entirely escape the baneful effects of Platonism, Scholasticism discovered the "worldliness of the world." See his "The Fathers, the Scholastics and Ourselves," *Communio*, XXIV, 2 (Summer, 1997), 380-394. More broadly, Balthasar has written extensively on the relevance of time as a theological category but this is developed quite differently from Lonergan's notion of differentiated consciousness. See, for example, Hans Urs Von Balthasar, *Word and Redemption,* Essays in Theology 2, Littledale, Dru (transl), (New York: Herder & Herder, 1965), *A Theological Anthropology,* (New York: Sheed and Ward, 1967) and, especially, *A Theology of History*, (New York: Sheed and Ward, 1963).

[21] Raymond Moloney, S.J., "The Mind of Christ in Transcendental Theology," in *Heythrop Journal*, XXV (1984), 292. He has returned to the issues of the present essay in his *The Knowledge of Christ*, (London and New York: Continuum, 1999).

[22]The foregoing paragraph is much indebted to Moloney, "The Mind of Christ in Transcendental Theology," 291–300, where Maloney draws on Lonergan's *De Verbo incarnato*. See also *Collection: Papers by Bernard Lonergan, S.J.* F.E. Crowe (ed), (London: Darton, Longman & Todd, 1967; New York: Herder and Herder, 1967), "Christ as Subject: A Reply (1959), especially 173–192. And see Daniel Helminiak, *The Same Jesus. A Contemporary Christology,* (Chicago: Loyola University Press, 1986), especially 138–149 and 198–208.

[23] Maloney, "The Mind of Christ in Transcendental Theology," 288–291,296.

[24] Lonergan, *Collection*, p. 196.

[25] Hans Urs Von Balthasar, *Theo-Drama, Theological Dramatic Theory, III. Dramatis Personae: Persons in Christ* (San Francisco: Ignatius Press, 1992), 150.

[26] "Christ as Subject: A Reply," 175-180.

[27] Mary Daly, *Beyond God the Father*, (Boston: Beacon Press, 1973); relevant here is Michelle Gonzalez, "Hans Urs Von Balthasar and Contemporary Feminist Theology," in *Theological Studies*, 65, 3 (September, 2004), 566-595. Some of her points may be found here and in Essay Four "The Church and Israel".

[28] *In Memory of Her: A Feminist Theological Reconstruction of Christian Origins,* (New York: Crossroad, 1983) and, more recently, *But She Said: Feminist Practices of Biblical Interpretation*, (Boston: Beacon Press, 1992).

[29] *God and the Rhetoric of Sexuality* (Philadelphia: Fortress Press, 1978).

[30] Some examples may suffice: from Plato: *Timaeus* 90e, 91a; *Laws* 5, 739c; from Aristotle: *Poetics* 15, 145a20; *Physics* 19, 192A13-14 (where woman is **aischron**, "shameful" while man is **kalon**, "beautiful").

[31]Leonardo Boff, *Ecclesiogenesis: The Base Communities Reinvent the Church*, (Maryknoll: Orbis, 1986). Here may be the place to observe that neither Lonergan nor Balthasar in my view are much represented in Liberation Theology but they are not far afield and their general relevance may come to light in Essay 13, "Christology and Ethics."

[32] Thomas Rourke has recently sounded the alarm against globalization in its current manifestation. See his "Contemporary Globalization: An Ethical and Anthropological Evaluation," *Communio*, 27 (Fall, 2000), 490-510.

[33] I am here very indebted to Daniel A. Helminiak, "Four Viewpoints on the Human: A Conceptual Schema for Interdisciplinary Studies: I," *Heythrop Journal*, XXVII (1986), 420-437and II, *Heythrop Journal,* XXVIII (1987), 1-15. In these pages, Helminiak takes up Lonergan's understanding of the higher viewpoints.

[34]Or perhaps the term spiritual development would be relevant. It may be defined as psychology within the philosophic viewpoint and as such the discipline that properly treats the spiritual. See Daniel Helminiak, *Spiritual Development. An Interdisciplinary Study,* (Chicago: Loyola University Press, 1987).

[35] Bernard J. Lonergan, S.J., *Method in Theology,* (London: Darton, Longman and Todd, 1972), 267-269.

[36] I refer the reader to my own article on which I draw heavily for the remarks to follow. See my "Some Contributions of Balthasar and Farrer on the Subject of Analogy of Being," *Downside Review*, 107, 368, (July, 1989), 183-190, but especially 184-186. I am here touching on the whole project of Balthasar's Theological Aesthetics which contains both his theology of Revelation and his fundamental theology.

[37] Essay Six, entitled "The Way to Nicea (325)", provides a context for this discussion.

[38] The literature on Gnosticism is truly vast and often quite specialized. Relevant just here is the monograph on Irenaeus by Hans Urs Von Balthasar, *The Glory of the Lord. A Theological Aesthetics. II.* "Studies in Theological Style: Clerical Styles," Andrew Louth et al. (trans), John Riches (ed) (San Francisco: Ignatius Press; New York: Crossroad, 1984), 31-94. I have written a small synopsis of its major points with some commentary in "Some Notes on the Interpretation of St. Irenaeus in the Works of Hans Urs Von Balthasar," *Studia Patristica*, XXIII, (1989), 284-288. An earlier anthology of Balthasar is also important: *Geduld des Reifens*, (Klosterberg, Basel: Verlag Benno Schwabe & Co., 1943) with a recent English translation by John Saward.

[39] Balthasar is known as a great interpreter of Greek theology. But he is also a thoughtful and insightful critic too. See his "The Fathers, the Scholastics and Ourselves" *Communio,* 372-380, where he critiques the unwelcome effects of Platonism on Christian mysticism and asceticism.

[40] Here I am following Balthasar very closely in his *The Christian State of Life,* (San Francisco: Ignatius Press, 1983). See also his "Christology And Ecclesial Obedience" in *Explorations in Theology,*IV: Spirit and Institution (San Francisco: Ignatius Press, 1995), especially 154-167.

[41] See Balthasar, *Explorations in Theology II: Spouse of the Word,* 319-331 on the laity and the Church.

[42] St. Augustine, *Confessions,* Henry Chadwick (transl), (Oxford, New York: Oxford University Press, 1992), 201.

[43] See my "A Note on Bonaventure's Appropriation of Augustine," *The Cord*, 42, 6, (June, 1992), 174-180.

[44] See Hans Urs Von Balthasar, "St. John of the Cross," *The Glory of the Lord. A Theological Aesthetics. III. Studies in Theological Style: Lay Styles,* (San Francisco: Ignatius Press, 1986), 105-171.

[45] I am drawing substantially for the whole essay on Hans Urs Von Balthasar, *Prayer*. Graham Harrison (transl), (San Francisco: Ignatius Press, 1986).

[46] In these paragraphs I have drawn generously from Bernard Lonergan, *Grace and Freedom: Operative Grace in the Thought of St. Thomas Aquinas*. J. Patout Burns (ed), (London: Darton, Longman & Todd, 1971; New York: Herder and Herder, 1971).

[47] I am very indebted in these sections to James M. Gustafson, *Christ and The Moral Life*, (New York: Harper & Row, 1968), especially chapter II. See also his *Can Ethics Be Christian?* (Chicago: The University of Chicago Press, 1975) and, more recently, *Ethics From a Theocentric Perspective*, 2 vol, (Chicago: University of Chicago Press, 1981-1984).

[48] Gustafson, *Christ and the Moral Life*, 130-137.

[49] Bernard Lonergan, S.J. *Insight,* (New York: Philosophical Library, 1963), 596. The balance of the essay adheres very closely to the text of *Insight.* Helpful too is Tad Dunne, S.J. *Lonergan and Spirituality: Towards a Spiritual Integration*, (Chicago: Loyola University Press, 1985), Chapter Three, "Acting" and Kenneth R. Melchin, *Living with Other People*, (Ottawa: St. Paul University/Novalis, Liturgical Press, 1998).

[50] Lonergan's understanding of the good of order is particularly helpful and promising. See *Method in Theology* on the Human Good, 27-55. In principle, this would be the point of connection between Lonergan (and, I might add, this essay) and many aspects of contemporary ethics, e.g., ecology, bioethics, social justice, feminist ethics, gay and gender issues, but these and related matters remain outside the present scope.

[51] Hans Urs Von Balthasar, *Theo-Drama, Theological Dramatic Theory, I: Prolegomena,* Graham Harrison (transl), (San Francisco: Ignatius Press, 1988), 125.

[52] I am here conveying my impressions in particular of *Theo-Drama, Theological Dramatic Theory, IV: The Action,* Graham Harrison (transl), (San Francisco: Ignatius Press, 1994).

[53] Balthasar here takes a page from Rene Girard. See *Theo-Drama, IV*, 300-310.

[54] *Theo-Drama, IV,* 317.

[55] Among the major works: For Lonergan, in addition to *Grace and Freedom,* there is *Verbum: Word and Idea in Aquinas,* David B. Burrell (ed), (Indiana: University of Notre Dame Press, 1967). A number of articles in *Collection* and *A Second Collection* and elsewhere treat of Thomas and of Thomism. For Balthasar, "Analogie und Dialektik" in *Divus Thomas,*22, (1944), 171-216; "Analogie und Natur" in *Divus Thomas*,23, (1945), 3-56; *Wahrheit*, (Einsiedeln: Benziger, 1947). *Wahrheit* is not strictly a historical study of Thomas, but he breathes a presence there. More to the point are the remarks on St. Thomas in *The Glory of the Lord, IV, The Realm of Metaphysics in Antiquity*, John Riches (ed), (San Francisco: Ignatius Press, 1989), 393-412. Balthasar's comments on St. Thomas are richly distributed across his work.

[56] Lonergan, *Method in Theology*, 4.

[57] I am chiefly drawing here on *Wahrheit.* And see Martin Bieler, "The Future of the Philosophy of Being," in *Communio*, 26, 3 (Fall, 1999), 455-485 (but especially 468-472).

BIBLIOGRAPHY

WORKS OF LONERGAN CITED

Lonergan, Bernard. "Christology Today: Methodological Reflections," *Le Christ hier, aujourd'hui, et demain*. Quebec: Les Presses de l'Universite Laval, 1976, 45-65.

Lonergan, Bernard. "The Transition from a Classicist World-View to Historical Mindedness," *A Second Collection.* London: Darton, Longman & Todd, 1974, 1-9.

Lonergan, Bernard. *The Way to Nicea*. London: Darton, Longman & Todd, 1976.

Lonergan, Bernard. *Method in Theology*. New York: Herder and Herder, 1972.

Lonergan, Bernard. "Christ as Subject: A Reply (1959)," *Collection: Papers by Bernard Lonergan, S.J.* F.E. Crowe (ed). London: Darton, Longman & Todd, 1967.

Lonergan, Bernard. *Grace and Freedom*. London: Darton, Longman & Todd, 1971.

Lonergan, Bernard. *Insight*. New York: Philosophical Library, 1963.

Lonergan, Bernard. Verbum: *Word and Idea in Aquinas*. Indiana: University of Notre Dame Press, 1967.

WORKS OF BALTHASAR CITED

Balthasar, Hans Urs Von. "Fides Christi," *Explorations in Theology II: Spouse of the Word*. San Francisco: Ignatius Press, 1991, 43-79.

Balthasar, Hans Urs Von. *You Have Words of Eternal Life*. San Francisco: Ignatius Press, 1991.

Balthasar, Hans Urs Von. *Theodrama. Theological Dramatic Theory. III. Dramatis Personae: Persons in Christ.* San Francisco: Ignatius Press, 1992.

Balthasar, Hans Urs Von. "The Mass, A Sacrifice of the Church?," *Explorations in Theology, III: Creator Spirit.* San Francisco: Ignatius Press, 1993, 185-243.

Balthasar, Hans Urs Von. "Christology and Ecclesial Obedience," *Explorations in Theology, IV: Spirit and Institution.* San Francisco: Ignatius Press, 1995, 139-167.

Balthasar, Hans Urs Von. *Mysterium Paschale*. Edinburgh: T&T Clark, 1990.

Balthasar, Hans Urs Von. *The Glory of the Lord. A Theological Aesthetics, II: Studies in Theological Style: Clerical Styles.* San Francisco: Ignatius Press, New York: Crossroad, 1984.

Balthasar, Hans Urs Von. "The Fathers, the Scholastics and Ourselves," in *Communio*, XXIV, 2 (Summer, 1997), 380-394.

Balthasar, Hans Urs Von. *A Theology of History*. New York: Sheed and Ward, 1963.

Balthasar, Hans Urs Von. *Word and Redemption*. New York: Herder & Herder, 1965.

Balthasar, Hans Urs Von. *A Theological Anthropology*. New York: Sheed and Ward, 1967.

Balthasar, Hans Urs Von. *Geduld des Reifens*. Kosterberg, Basel: Verlag Benno Schwabe & Co., 1943.
Balthasar, Hans Urs Von. *The Christian State of Life*. San Francisco: Ignatius Press, 1983.
Balthasar, Hans Urs Von. *The Glory of the Lord. A Theological Aesthetics. III. Studies in Theological Style: Lay Styles*. San Francisco: Ignatius Press, 1986.
Balthasar, Hans Urs Von. *Theo-Drama, Theological Dramatic Theory, I: Prolegomena*. San Francisco: Ignatius Press, 1988.
Balthasar, Hans Urs Von. *Theo-Drama, Theological Dramatic Theory, IV: The Action*. San Francisco: Ignatius Press, 1994.
Balthasar, Hans Urs Von. "Analogie und Dialektik," in *Divus Thomas*, 22 (1944), 171-216.
Balthasar, Hans Urs Von. "Analogie und Natur," in *Divus Thomas*, 23 (1945), 3-56.
Balthasar, Hans Urs Von. *Wahrheit*. Einsiedeln: Benziger, 1947.
Balthasar, Hans Urs Von. *The Glory of the Lord, IV, The Realm of Metaphysics in Antiquity*. San Francisco: Ignatius Press, 1989.
Balthasar, Hans Urs Von. *Prayer*. San Francisco: Ignatius Press, 1986.

OTHER WORKS CITED

Bettenson, Henry (ed*). Documents of the Christian Church*. London: Oxford University Press, 1967.
Bieler, Martin. "The Future of the Philosophy of Being," in *Communio*, 26, 3 (Fall, 1999), 455-485.
St. Augustine. *Confessions*. Oxford, New York: Oxford University Press, 1992.
Boff, Leonardo. *Ecclesiogenesis: The Base Communities Reinvent the Church*. Maryknoll: Orbis, 1986.
Brown, Raymond. *The Death of the Messiah*, II Vols. New York: Doubleday, 1994.
Daly, Mary. *Beyond God the Father*. Boston: Beacon Press, 1973.
Doran, Robert M. "Lonergan and Balthasar: Methodological Considerations," in *Theological Studies,* 58, 1 (March, 1997), 61-84.
Doran, Robert M. "Bernard Lonergan and the Functions of Systematic Theology," in *Theological Studies,* 59, 49 (December, 1998), 569-607.
Dunne, Tad. *Lonergan and Spirituality: Towards a Spiritual Integration*. Chicago: Loyola University Press, 1985.
Eusebius. *Ecclesiastical History, Books IX, X*. Vol II. Cambridge: Harvard University Press, 1973.
Fessio, Joseph. *The Origin of the Church in Christ's Kenosis: The Ontological Structure of the Church in the Ecclesiology of Hans Urs Von Balthasar*. Dissertation: University of Regensburg, 1974.
Fiorenza, Elizabeth Schüssler. *In Memory of Her: A Feminist Theological Reconstruction of Christian Origins*. New York: Crossroad, 1983.
Fiorenza, Elizabeth Schüssler. *But She Said: Feminist Practices of Biblical Interpretation*. Boston: Beacon Press, 1992.

Gonzalez, Michelle. "Hans Urs Von Balthasar and Contemporary Feminist Theology," in *Theological Studies*, 65, 3 (September, 2004), 566-595.

Grillmeier, Aloys. *Christ in Christian Tradition, I.* Atlanta: John Knox Press, 1975.

Gustafson, James M. *Christ and the Moral Life.* New York: Harper & Row, 1968.

Gustafson, James M. *Can Ethics Be Christian?* Chicago: The University of Chicago Press, 1975.

Gustafson, James M. *Ethics From Theocentric Perspective,* 2Vols. Chicago: University of Chicago Press, 1981-1984.

Helminiak, Daniel. *The Same Jesus. A Contemporary Christology.* Chicago: Loyola University Press, 1986.

Helminiak, Daniel. *Spiritual Development. An Interdisciplinary Study.* Chicago: Loyola University Press, 1987.

Helminiak, Daniel. "Four Viewpoints on the Human: A Conceptual Schema for Interdisciplinary Studies, I," in *Heythrop Journal*, XXVII (1986), 420-437.

Helminiak, Daniel. "Four Viewpoints on the Human: A Conceptual Schema for Interdisciplinary Studies, II," in *Heythrop Journal*, XXVIII (1987), 1-15.

Hunt, Anne. "Psychological Analogy and Paschal Mystery in Trinitarian Theology," in *Theological Studies,* 59, 2 (June, 1998), 197-218.

Jaeger, Werner. *Early Christianity and Greek Paideia.* London, Oxford, New York: Oxford University Press, 1969.

Kehl, Medard, Loser, Werner (eds*). The Von Balthasar Reader.* New York: Crossroad, 1982.

Lewis, Bradley V. "Globalization And The Eclipse of Natural Right: What We Might Learn From Plato And The Other Greeks," in *Communio*, 27 (2000), 431-463.

Lamb, Matthew. *History, Method and Theology. A Dialectical Comparison of Wilhelm Dilthey's Critique of Historical Reason and Bernard Lonergan's Meta-Methodology.* Missoula: Scholars Press, 1978.

Melchin, Kenneth R. *Living with Other People.* Ottawa: St. Paul University/Novalis Press, The Liturgical Press, 1998.

Moloney, Raymond. "The Mind of Christ in Transcendental Theology: Rahner, Lonergan and Crowe," in *Heythrop Journal*, XXV (1984), 288-300.

Moloney, Raymond. *The Knowledge of Christ.* London and New York: Continuum, 1999.

Mooney, Hilary A. *The Liberation of Consciousness: Bernard Lonergan's Theological Foundations in Dialogue with the Theological Aesthetics of Hans Urs von Balthasar.* Frankfurt: Josef Knecht, 1992.

Prestige, G.L. *Fathers And Heretics.* London: SPCK, 1940.

Rourke, Thomas R. "Contemporary Globalization: An Ethical and Anthropological Evaluation," in *Communio* XXVII, 3 (Fall, 2000), 490-510.

Snell, Bruno. *The Discovery of Mind. The Greek Origins of European Thought.* Cambridge: Harvard University Press, 1953.

Tortorelli, Kevin. "Some Contributions of Balthasar and Farrer on the Subject of Analogy of Being," in *Downside Review*, 107, 368 (July, 1989), 183-190.

Tortorelli, Kevin. "Some Notes on the Interpretation of St. Irenaeus in the Works of Hans Urs Von Balthasar," in *Studia Patristica*, XXIII (1989), 284-288.

Tortorelli, Kevin. "A Note on Bonaventure's Appropriation of Augustine," in *The Cord*, 42, 6 (June, 1992), 174-180.
Tortorelli, Kevin. "Some Methods of Interpretation in St. Irenaeus," in *Vetera Christianorum*, 30 (1993), 123-132.
Trible, Phyllis. *God and the Rhetoric of Sexuality.* Philadelphia: Fortress Press, 1978.

1. BIBLICAL INDEX

Old Testament

New Testament

2. GENERAL INDEX